COMMUNITIES OF PRACTICE

Communities of Practice

An Alaskan Native Model for Language Teaching and Learning

EDITED BY PATRICK E. MARLOW
AND SABINE SIEKMANN

THE UNIVERSITY OF ARIZONA PRESS
TUCSON

THE UNIVERSITY OF ARIZONA PRESS

www.uapress.arizona.edu

Library of Congress Cataloging-in-Publication Data

Communities of practice : an Alaskan native model for language teaching and learning / edited by Patrick E. Marlow and Sabine Siekmann.
p. cm.
Includes bibliographical references and index.
ISBN 978-0-8165-3016-8 (pbk. : alk. paper) 1. Alaska natives—Languages—Study and teaching. 2. Alaska natives—Education. 3. Indigenous peoples—Study and teaching. 4. Second language acquisition—Study and teaching. 5. Education, Bilingual—Alaska. 6. Bilingualism in children—Alaska. I. Marlow, Patrick E., 1966– II. Siekmann, Sabine. III. Alaska Native Language Center.
PM501.A4C66 2013
497'.1—dc23

2012036966

Publication of this book is made possible in part by the proceeds of a permanent endowment created with the assistance of a Challenge Grant from the National Endowment for the Humanities, a federal agency.

Manufactured in the United States of America on acid-free, archival-quality paper containing a minimum of 30% post-consumer waste and processed chlorine free.

18 17 16 15 14 13 6 5 4 3 2 1

Contents

Acknowledgments

We acknowledge the help and support throughout this project of our regional grant partners and their representatives: Vivian Korthius of the Association of Village Council Presidents; Abby Augustine, Gayle Miller, Nita Rearden, and Bev Williams of the Lower Kuskokwim School District; Cheryl Jerabek of the Kuspuk School District; and William Beans, John Lamont, and Joanna Wassillie of the Lower Yukon School District. If it were not for their personal commitment, the Second Language Acquisition Teacher Education (SLATE) project would not have come into being.

We also acknowledge the administrative help and support of the University of Alaska Fairbanks's Linguistics Program, Alaska Native Language Center, School of Education, and Kuskokwim Campus, including the editorial assistance provided by Leon Unruh of Alaska Native Language Center Press. Finally, we acknowledge the generous financial support of the US Department of Education Alaska Native Education Program (#S35A060055).

Finally, we thank the SLATE sisters for their energy, enthusiasm, and occasional reality checks throughout the project. Your personal commitment, drive, and dedication inspired us all. You are what it is all about.

Prologue

Community of Practice

The idea for the book, its focus, and structure came out of countless discussions among the Second Language Acquisition Teacher Education (SLATE)faculty: Marilee Coles-Ritchie, Patrick E. Marlow, Sabine Siekmann, and Joan Parker Webster. The various chapters developed out of discussions and collaborations among the faculty as well as between the faculty and doctoral candidates Walkie Charles, April G. L. Counceller, Theresa Arevgaq John, and Hishinlai' "Kathy R. Sikorski."

From the beginning of this project, the faculty set out to engage the SLATE students in ways that would deepen their understanding of second language acquisition and teaching and prepare them for leadership roles in both Yup'ik and English-language programming within their own K–12 or university context. As we hope this volume can attest, the direction of the engagement, the deepening of the understanding, and with it the sense of responsibility to act, was not something that only the students experienced.

One SLATE graduate, Atan (Veronica Michael), concluded her thesis by honoring her grandfather with the words "I hope I have told a good enough story" (Michael 2010, p. 89). Atan invoked the traditional roles of storyteller and active listener. As the storyteller, the writer of her thesis, she hoped she had done her grandparents honor by sharing accurately and compassionately her own story and that of her ancestors, her community, and her research participants, two Yugtun-speaking mothers struggling to keep the Yugtun language and culture alive within their own families. She also hoped that she had told a story that, like the ones her grandfather told, would be worthy of her many audiences and help them better understand their own situations. Like Atan, we, too, hope we have told a good enough story.

COMMUNITIES OF PRACTICE

Introduction

Patrick E. Marlow, Marilee Coles-Ritchie,
Sabine Siekmann, and Joan Parker Webster

As Indigenous language communities struggle with language loss, many scholars (Hinton & Hale 2001; Johnson & Swain 1997) and community activists (Kipp 2000) now recognize immersion education as the primary means of restoring Indigenous[1] and other heritage[2] languages to community use. In the Alaskan context, Indigenous languages are limited to the twenty identified Alaska Native languages and their dialects. Heritage languages include both Alaska Native and immigrant languages. The dominant language is English.

In Alaska, immersion programs are not the only or even the most common program type in place in public school contexts. Given the relatively small number of heritage language teachers and the complex issues involved in language maintenance and revitalization, creating any heritage language program within the public education system—let alone an immersion program—is a daunting task. This task is made all the more difficult by the lack of local professional development opportunities for potential language teachers.

Of course, two nationally recognized programs offer professional development opportunities for heritage language teachers. The University of Minnesota's Center for Advanced Research in Language Acquisition (CARLA) and the University of Arizona's American Indian Language Development Institute (AILDI) offer opportunities for heritage language teachers to develop their expertise through summer programs. However, neither of these excellent programs is tailored to the Alaskan context. The CARLA summer institutes offer courses in immersion education and other relevant topics in language teaching; however, classes focus largely on foreign language and English as a second language (ESL) instruction. The unique situation of Indigenous languages is not well represented in these courses. AILDI, on the other hand, was specifically designed for Indigenous language teachers, yet the program does not lead to advanced degrees. The Second Language Acquisition Teacher Education (SLATE) program at the University of Alaska Fairbanks is intended to be a bridge between these two approaches. By focusing on the specific needs of heritage language teachers and distance education, program faculty hope to build on the strengths of these and other nationally recognized programs and provide a workable model for other contexts.

One challenge for an Alaskan program tailored exclusively to heritage language teachers is the small number of candidates. Such a narrow focus could make such a program unsustainable by excluding candidates interested in English-language programming. That is why we decided to develop a broader program that would allow both heritage and English language teachers an important opportunity to develop common understandings concerning second language acquisition, language teaching, and bilingualism. Such understandings, we hope, will allow heritage and English language teachers to work together to foster their students' success in both languages. Through this model, they would be able to situate themselves in a more global context based on current notions of multilingualism within the frameworks of sociocultural theory and critical pedagogy.

The purpose of this book is to share how the SLATE program, initially funded through a US Department of Education grant, was developed and implemented based on the stated goals of (1) improving Yup'ik and English education in Alaska's Yup'ik region, (2) enabling local leadership in language programming, and (3) fostering community-driven research. Perhaps more important, it is also a story about how the initial cohort of English and Yup'ik language teachers from southwestern Alaska negotiated and ultimately completed the SLATE program and personally added to the accomplishment of these goals.

Each chapter bridges theoretical concepts underlying second-language teaching and learning to practical applications in classrooms populated with linguistically and culturally diverse students. The larger theoretical frameworks informing our work are sociocultural theory and critical pedagogy. By "sociocultural theory," we first refer to the work of theorists and researchers (e.g., Heath 1983, 1986; Norton 2000; Norton & Toohey 2004; Ochs 1988) situated within the broader sociocultural domain. In this view, sociocultural theory is concerned with socialization and the discursive nature of the construction of identities (e.g., gender, Native, child). We also use the phrase to refer to the work of Lev Vygotsky and theorists and researchers engaged in applied linguistics research (e.g., Appel & Lantolf 1994; Lantolf 2000; Lantolf & Thorne 2006; Swain 2000; Thorne 2005). As such, sociocultural theory is also a framework that focuses on how culturally formed and socially enacted meanings influence the development of mental activity.

By "critical pedagogy," we refer to the interactive relationship between teaching and learning and theory and practice, termed *praxis*, developed by Paolo Freire (2000 [1968]). This relationship reflects a transformative process that can help us challenge and reflect on our long-held assumptions about what we view as the status quo. Thus, this active transformative process can help us question our theories about and practices in the world and act on them. Drawing from the work of Antonia Darder, Joe Kincheloe, Peter McLaren, bell hooks, and others, we further construct our own critical pedagogy that underlies the theory and practices developed in this book. Our theory and practices are based on these principles:

- Use local knowledge and practices.
- Enable students to become critical producers of meanings and texts.
- Provide tools that can help students critically question systems of cultural domination and transform themselves from objects to subjects, passive to active.
- Illuminate the relations among knowledge, authority, and power.

Additional concepts that are particularly germane to our context of mentoring distance students working with(in) Indigenous communities and that link these theoretical frameworks to our practical application are dialogic engagement, joint collaborative activity, intersubjectivity, community action research, and insider/outsider research. The theoretical framework laid out in this introduction will be further developed, re(de)fined and recast in each subsequent chapter as it is linked to real-life applications, such as establishing truly collaborative models for making decisions about grant management, defining the curriculum and delivery model, identifying research questions and appropriate research methodologies, and creating mentoring relationships.

Comment on Usage

Throughout the text we capitalize the term *Indigenous*. This is done to acknowledge that Indigenous peoples are seen and understood on a par with other ethnocultural groups, whether defined broadly (e.g., Europeans, Americans) or narrowly (e.g., Swedes, Japanese).

The term *Yup'ik* refers to Central Alaskan Yup'ik people as an ethnic and cultural group. It is also used as a modifier when referring to the cultural practices of Yup'ik people (e.g., Yup'ik culture) or when referring to school practices (e.g., Yup'ik-medium instruction, Yup'ik immersion). Whenever possible we use the term *Yugtun* to refer to the language itself (e.g., speakers of Yugtun, speaking Yugtun). However, the use of the Indigenous term for the language itself is not yet common practice. Therefore, the term *Yup'ik* or *Yup'ik language* may also appear, especially in quotations within the text.

The term *student* generally refers to graduate students. However, we prefer the term *teachers* when speaking of the SLATE master's participants in particular as all are themselves K–12 teachers.

Throughout the book, surnames are preferred over first names when referring to the teachers, the doctoral students, and the faculty. Although the use of first names might be more in keeping with the nature of the project, this preference is based on a desire to acknowledge and cite the work of all project participants equally, whether the work is published or unpublished, written or oral.

Organization of This Book

In Chapter 1, we briefly describe the Central Yup'ik context and the evolution of the SLATE program. Within this evolution, we discuss participant recruitment, as well as our approach to research and course content. The discussion of research includes an overview of the Graduate Research Collaboratives (GRCs), a central design element in the SLATE project. Finally, we introduce the teachers who were the primary participants in this project.

Chapter 2 extends the concept of the GRC model by focusing on the aspect of mentoring. The chapter uses data highlighting the students' experiences as teachers/learners and mentors.

Chapters 3 through 6 focus on the classes taught during the 2008 intensive summer session. In Chapter 3, Sabine Siekmann and Hishinlai' "Kathy R. Sikorski" discuss the curriculum and materials development course. In Chapter 4, Joan Parker Webster and Theresa Arevgaq John discuss their multiliteracies course. In Chapter 5, Marilee Coles-Ritchie and Walkie Charles discuss the course on assessment. Finally, in Chapter 6,

Patrick E. Marlow and April G. L. Counceller discuss the course on language policy and planning. Each of these chapters approaches what was taught from the perspectives of planning, implementation, and reflection on course content, format, and student projects, with a discussion of lessons learned and adaptations to other contexts.

The final chapter derives from a single three-day summative program evaluation session held in November 2010. With the project largely complete, the faculty discussed the successes and challenges of the program and reflected on what might have been done differently and what the next steps might be. Thus, the chapter provides a forum for the faculty to discuss their efforts to build a community of learners through research and reflect on multiple definitions of success.

Finally, the book ends with a brief epilogue in which we attempt to answer the important questions: Where have the SLATE graduates gone? How and in what ways is this important work continuing?

Notes

1. We use Wilson's (2008, p. 34) meaning for the term *Indigenous languages*, which refers to the languages of people who claim ancestry from the original inhabitants of a country or territory.

2. We use the term *heritage language* to refer to a language spoken or formerly spoken in the home environment or familial context that differs from the surrounding dominant language.

CHAPTER ONE

SLATE Context and History

Patrick E. Marlow and Sabine Siekmann

Linguistic Context

Central Yup'ik is traditionally spoken throughout southwestern Alaska, from Norton Sound to Bristol Bay, an area covering more than 112,000 square miles (roughly the size of Arizona; see Figure 1.1). More densely populated in comparison to the rest of Alaska's Indigenous populations, the "Yup'ik region" has a combined census of 23,000 Yup'ik Eskimos scattered in more than sixty villages. Transportation within the region is limited to plane, boat, and snowmobile, because none of the villages are connected by road. Unemployment averages around 16 percent, and nearly 59 percent of schoolchildren within the region live below the poverty line.

Although more than 60 percent of schoolchildren in this region are classified as limited English proficient by current Alaska state standards, less than a quarter of all Yup'ik villages—mainly those on the lower Kuskokwim River, on Nelson Island, and between these two landmarks—have a majority of children growing up with Yup'ik as their first language. In nearly all other villages, a local variety of English, heavily influenced by contact with Yup'ik, is the first language of most if not all children. Although nearly half the Yup'ik Eskimo population speaks Yup'ik natively, outside of what is now the "linguistic heartland" (see Figure 1.2), the average age of the youngest speakers now ranges from approaching thirty to approaching fifty (Krauss 1997, p. 6). There is great variation from village to village, but in some villages—especially those in the Yukon Delta and Bristol Bay regions—only the grandparental generations still speak the language.

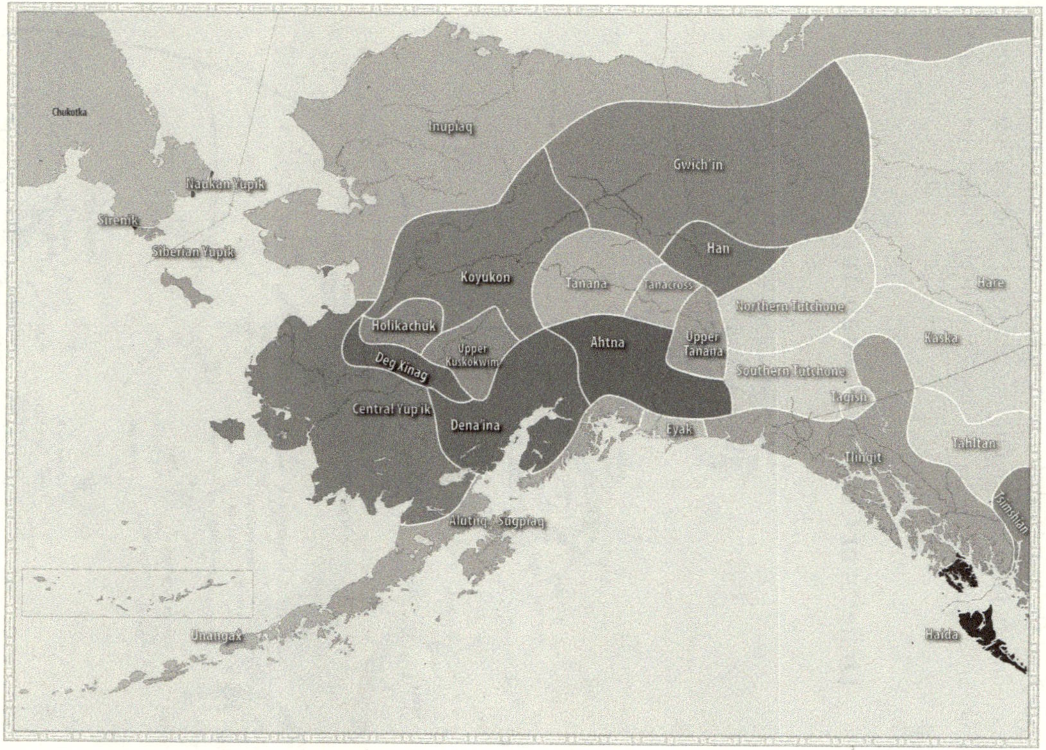

Figure 1.1. Alaska Native languages (source: http://www.uaf.edu/anlc/)

As Figure 1.2 indicates, Central Yup'ik forms a dialect continuum with five major dialects (from north to south): Norton Sound, General Central Yup'ik (GCY), Hooper Bay–Chevak, Nunivak, and Egegik.[1] Within these, Jacobson (1998) further divides Norton Sound into Unaliq and Kotlik subdialects, and GCY is divided into Peripheral and Core subdialects. Finally, according to Jacobson, "a number of lexical (and to a lesser extent, phonological) features cut across dialect and subdialect boundaries" (1998, p. xii).

Dialects of Central Alaskan Yup'ik

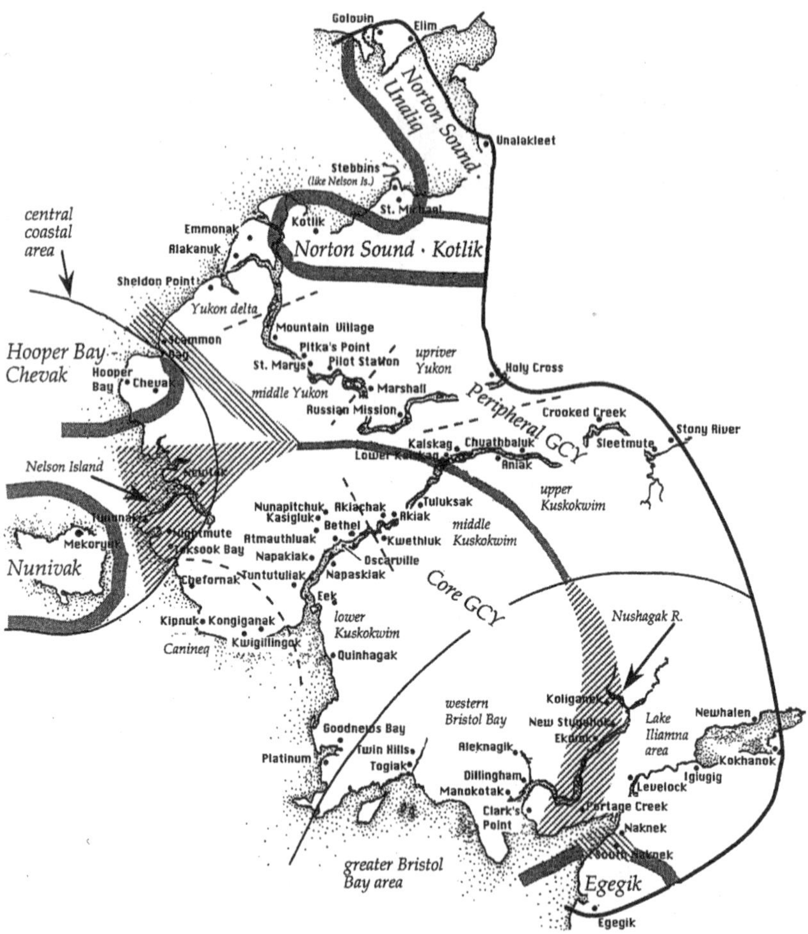

Figure 1.2. Dialects of Central Alaskan Yup'ik (adapted from Jacobson 1998, p. xiii)

In this sociolinguistic context, it is not surprising that a broad range of Yup'ik language programs have developed within the more than sixty schools and nine school districts in the region. Since the beginning of Yup'ik-medium education in 1968 (Marlow 2004; Orvik 1975; Reed 1974), schools, school districts, and universities have worked to overcome personnel shortages and meet the needs of evolving Yup'ik language programs. At the time of this writing, program types range from language and culture enrichment programs, to transitional bilingual programs designed to facilitate acquisition of English by Native speakers of Yup'ik, to Yup'ik immersion programs designed to facilitate the acquisition of Yup'ik as an ancestral language where that language is all but lost, to dual-language development programs intended to foster the academic development of both Yup'ik and English. Unfortunately, although a handful of communities have teachers fluent in Yup'ik and experienced in language pedagogy, few have personnel familiar with immersion education, and some (especially those in the Yukon Delta and Bristol Bay regions) lack even teacher aides proficient in Yup'ik.

The Evolution of the SLATE Program

In 2006, the Second Language Acquisition Teacher Education (SLATE) emphasis within the master of arts in applied linguistics (University of Alaska Fairbanks) was created. The SLATE program, under the auspices of US Department of Education grant funds, included program development (partner meetings, faculty time) as well as student support (tuition, fees, travel) for four Alaska Native doctoral candidates and up to twenty MA candidates from three partnered school districts (Lower Kuskokwim, Lower Yukon, and Kuspuk) within the Yup'ik region. Given the relatively small population base and the broad range of program types and language needs and goals within the targeted region and the state, we sought to establish a fairly broad graduate program that included heritage and English-language teachers.

With the many goals and multiple audiences for the SLATE program, we spent more than a year working with local community and district representatives to develop the relevant coursework, appropriate delivery model, compatible research paradigm, and an equitable recruitment process. In the summer of 2007, eighteen masters students began their coursework. By fall 2010, all completed the program and graduated with a master's degree.

Recruitment

Program partners jointly established a recruitment process that included both an academic and a community evaluation of potential candidates. This dual-evaluation approach was guided by experience that told us reliance on only one measure would likely result in teachers dropping out of the program either because they were not academically strong enough or because they did not have the drive and community support necessary to stick with a challenging program. Therefore, the application process required potential students to provide a statement of personal and professional goals, three letters of reference (a community letter, a job letter, and an academic letter), and full academic transcripts. Faculty reviewed transcripts, personal statements, and letters for evidence that the student could succeed in an academic program. Partner representatives looked primarily at the letters of reference and personal statement to assess the person's commitment to language teaching within the community and the likelihood that the person would (on completion of the program) contribute in meaningful ways to the ongoing development of local language programming. Faculty and community recommendations were given equal weight in the final selection process. Reflecting on this process, we find it clear that this collaboration between university faculty, school representatives, and community members was crucial to ensuring individual student success and ultimately the overall success of the SLATE program.

Development of the GRC Model

In an effort to foster collaborative research, we organized candidates into four research cohorts called Graduate Research Collaboratives (GRCs). Each GRC focused on a general area of research (pedagogy, multiliteracies, assessment, and language policy and planning). One faculty member headed each GRC, and each GRC consisted of one Alaska Native doctoral candidate and up to six MA candidates. GRC meetings were initially held biweekly and later, as research agendas solidified, weekly. These regular meetings facilitated the development of individual and group research agendas and allowed for ongoing conversations and exchanges among peers, doctoral students, and faculty members. In an effort to connect course content directly to research, faculty encouraged MA candidates to adapt individual course assignments directly to their intended research.

The GRC model was inspired by lab-based research. Traditional physical science research is often done in a lab setting with multiple graduate students working on overlapping and usually highly coordinated research. In the physical sciences, the advantages to such a model include (1) the ability to approach the research on multiple, coordinated fronts with different students looking at different parts of the problem and building on each other's results; and (2) the opportunity for more experienced graduate students to mentor newer students in terms of the expectations of graduate school and the research field. Emulating the lab model, each GRC included a cohort of between three and six MA candidates; each focused on a general area of research (pedagogy, multiliteracies, assessment, and language policy and planning); each was headed by a faculty member; and each included an Alaska Native doctoral candidate as near-peer mentor. Although inspired by it, the GRC model differs significantly from a faculty-centered hierarchical lab structure in which students carry out predefined research on questions established by the faculty member or group leader.

Within the SLATE project, the faculty were well aware of their positioning as well as their strengths and weaknesses. None of the faculty were community members. To varying degrees, all were "outsiders" working within an Indigenous context. As such, we claimed varying degrees of experience but no expertise in Alaska Native or Yup'ik ways of knowing and doing things. Similarly, the doctoral students were Alaska Native, but only two (Charles and John) were Yup'ik. Counceller was Alutiiq, a closely related Eskimo language/cultural group, and Sikorski was Gwich'in, an Alaskan Athabascan language/cultural group. Two of the faculty (Parker Webster and Coles-Ritchie) were experienced K–12 teachers, but neither had taught in southwestern Alaska, and many of the MA/MEd candidates claimed more years of experience in K–12 classrooms. Furthermore, many of the master's degree candidates were well respected and knowledgeable community members, some approaching the status of elders within their own communities. Thus, the GRC model was established with the full knowledge that everyone would have the opportunity to be a more experienced peer on a variety of topics. This constant shifting of perspectives and relationships within each GRC is in stark contrast to the top-down, faculty-centered hierarchical lab structure that inspired it.

Content

The program requirements are similar to existing applied linguistics/ Teachers of English as a Second or Other Language (TESOL) programs throughout the nation. The SLATE program was designed to meet the specific needs of teachers serving Yup'ik language speakers and learners through (1) the addition of specific coursework to help candidates understand and investigate issues relevant to them, their communities, and their schools; (2) modification of course content to focus on second language acquisition of children, bilingualism, and issues of language, culture, and identity in language learning; and (3) establishment of a delivery model that integrates teaching and research.

The establishment of the SLATE specialization within an existing MA in applied linguistics program was one of our major accomplishments during the first year of the grant. While the list of proposed courses was based on existing applied linguistics/TESOL programs, the curriculum was vetted with the partners in an extended retreat. During this retreat, the grant partners and representatives of three partnered school districts and one Native organization finalized the course offerings required for grant-funded participants. This is one example of the commitment to true university–school–community collaborations that characterizes the conceptual framework underlying our efforts both in teaching and research.

SPECIFIC COURSEWORK. Within the Yup'ik context (as well as the Alaska Native context more generally), it was necessary to address the complex questions of language loss, language revitalization, and the appropriate roles of English and Yup'ik (and other Alaska Native languages) in modern society. With more communities turning to immersion programs in attempts to address these issues (a third of SLATE candidates were immersion teachers or administrators), it was necessary for SLATE to address the specific needs and concerns of immersion schools in the Alaska context.

Although issues of language loss and language revitalization are addressed through most of the coursework, one class in particular is dedicated to these topics. In Language Policy and Planning (a course not found in the majority of applied linguistics programs across the nation) candidates are exposed to a variety of models describing and addressing language loss and revitalization (e.g., Fishman 1991; Hinton & Hale 2001; Krauss 1992; Paulston 1994). In addition, candidates explore the history and current state of US and Alaska language policy and the intimate tie between that policy and bilingual education (e.g., Alton 1998; Cooper 1989; Crawford 2004; Marlow 2004). These topics are essential to understanding the Alaskan educational context.

In another course designed specifically for the SLATE program, Multiliteracies, candidates extend the notion of literacy beyond the written word to include oral narratives, visual performance, and song and dance.

This broadening is particularly relevant to our context, as Yup'ik culture is grounded in an oral tradition involving not only storytelling but also expression through dance and song. The immersion schools in particular base their curriculum on Yup'ik values and ways of life, in which these forms of literacy are of central importance.

MODIFICATION OF COURSE CONTENT. In addition to the two unique courses just described, we tailored the content of each course to address the specific needs of heritage language teachers in a variety of language programs. In the context of language loss and revitalization within which the language programs in the Yup'ik region operate, the focus for the courses Second Language Acquisition and Methods of Second Language Teaching was naturally on the processes of child second language acquisition in immersion and other instructed settings, rather than on adults learning in a naturalistic setting. Because one of the overarching goals of Yup'ik language programs is to allow students to make the most of opportunities at home in the village and "outside" in majority culture communities, discussion in several of the courses (e.g., Second Language Acquisition, Materials Development, Assessment for the Second Language Classroom) centered on bilingualism: types of bilingualism; cognitive and social effects of bilingualism; factors fostering bilingualism; instructional models fostering bilingualism; bilingualism, code-switching, and language loss; and bilingualism and bidialecticism. A third theme incorporated into the SLATE program more so than in similar programs nationally and internationally is an emphasis on the connection between language, culture, and identity in language learning in several courses (e.g., Multiliteracies, Language Policy and Planning, Second Language Acquisition).

INTEGRATION OF TEACHING AND RESEARCH. A strictly traditional model (assuming full-time, on-campus study, isolated research agendas) will not work for the sociolinguistic context described earlier. Any program must recognize that Alaska Native students historically have had difficulty completing graduate degrees, partly because they are place bound, residing in isolated villages accessible only by plane, boat, or snowmobile. In addition, our experience working with Alaska Native students suggests that many prefer collaborative learning environments. This preference may compound the relative isolation of the student, further hampering degree completion. In an effort to overcome these obstacles, SLATE integrated teaching and research into its course delivery model using summer intensives, distance education courses, and the GRC research cohorts.

We held the first summer intensive in July 2007. Because this was the first summer for teachers in the program, coursework focused on introducing them to the field of second language acquisition and the range of research methods they were likely to employ. To facilitate the development of research questions and begin defining methodologies, a poster session was held at the end of the summer intensive. Simulating a poster session typical of many research conferences, each teacher prepared and presented a poster illustrating her initial proposal for the intended research project.

The following fall, the teachers enrolled in one research credit and a general overview of linguistic analysis. The research credit provided faculty with a way to formalize weekly GRC meetings and, through those meetings, assist the teachers in defining their research agendas. The following spring the pattern was repeated, and all teachers enrolled in one research credit as well as a course in second language teaching methods. To foster a sense of a Yup'ik language teacher cohort, and to allow for collaborative dialogue in the Yup'ik language among them, the teaching methods course was split into two sections, one for Yup'ik language teachers and one for English language teachers.

By summer 2008, the teachers had defined their research through a formal proposal, and many had begun data collection. Our goal for the summer intensive was to help the teachers focus their research and develop additional expertise in their research area. We divided the teachers into two cohorts and enrolled each cohort in coursework specific to their GRCs. Cohort 1 included the eleven teachers participating in either the Pedagogy or Multiliteracies GRC. Teachers in cohort 1 took a curriculum and materials development and a multiliteracies course. Cohort 2 included the seven teachers participating in either the Assessment or Language Policy and Planning GRC. Teachers in cohort 2 took an assessment and a language policy and planning course. A more detailed description of these cohorts is given later. Because of the success of the previous year's poster session, we organized a student miniconference for the last day of the 2008 summer intensive and invited faculty, administrators, and students from across the university. Students presented their work in a variety of formats, including posters, multimedia presentations, and portfolios.

In fall 2008, the teachers took the eighth and final content course required for their degree. Cohort 1 enrolled in a language assessment course, and Cohort 2 enrolled in a curriculum and materials development course. Originally, we had hoped for both cohorts to complete all the available courses. However, this would have added an additional three credits to the basic requirements for the MA in applied linguistics, and in all likelihood it would have delayed degree completion for all the teachers. Therefore, in spring 2009 teachers took an additional research methods course. This course was divided into four sections, with each faculty member responsible for his or her own GRC. The goal for this course was to review research methodology to facilitate thesis completion.

We held the third and final summer intensive in July 2009, with a focus on data analysis and thesis writing. Although none of the teachers were ready to defend by the end of July, all had completed drafts of one or more key chapters (e.g., research methodology, literature review, data analysis). The grant supporting the program was due to expire at the end of August, but we had sufficient funds for a no-cost extension to provide tuition, fees, and some travel support for the 2009–2010 academic year. Throughout the fall semester, the teachers continued to work on their thesis and project drafts in their GRCs, and the first defense was held in Bethel in November 2009. Subsequent defenses were held in February and April 2010. Of the eighteen master's-level participants, seventeen graduated in May and one graduated in August 2010.

The Participants and Setting of This Book

As noted earlier, the goal for the summer 2008 intensive was to help the teachers focus their research and develop additional expertise in their research area.

Cohort 1

Cohort 1, which consisted of teachers in the Pedagogy and Multiliteracies GRCs, included nine Yup'ik and two non-Native MA/MEd candidates. Seven were Yup'ik first-language speakers, and two were monolingual English speakers. At the time, five were teaching in English-medium schools and four in Yup'ik-medium schools; two were teaching Yup'ik as a second language.

- Nine teachers are of Yup'ik descent.
- Seven are Yup'ik first-language speakers.
- Age range: 29–59 years (mean 41.8, median 40).
- Five teach in English-medium schools, four teach in Yup'ik-medium schools, two teach Yup'ik as a second language

PEDAGOGY. Cathy Moses is a third-grade teacher in a Yup'ik Language Development Program. Yup'ik Language Development is a K–3 transitional bilingual program in which children are taught literacy and most content area skills in Yup'ik, before transitioning to English in the third grade. In her letter of application, Moses explained that after more than fifteen years of classroom experience, hearing her students speak Yugtun still "warms my heart." This is in part because her own educational experience growing up was very different. She writes in her letter of application: "I remember my first days of school where I had no clue as to what the English teacher was saying. I had to rely mostly on his nonverbal cues and on the help of my sister and close friends. It was during that time I believe I became very observant of people and their actions. I gauged my atmosphere as safe and somewhat unsafe based on the attitudes and the surrounding atmosphere."

Though the children entering Moses's classroom are still relatively proficient in Yup'ik, continuing language shift means they are exhibiting some of the characteristics Merrill Swain and Robert Keith Johnson (1997) describe for immersion settings, such as high levels of proficiency in listening comprehension and oral fluency but problems with accuracy. In her thesis, Moses identified a specific ending, *mun/nun*, "to," as a problematic area for her students. To improve accuracy with this ending, she employed a story-based approach. After identifying a story that employed this structure in a central way, she engaged the students in a series of form-focused activities and looked for improved accuracy in their written expression (Moses 2010).

When Carol Oulton joined the SLATE program, she was a kindergarten teacher at Ayaprun Elitnaurvak, a Yup'ik immersion school in Bethel. She had been teaching in the Yup'ik-medium classroom for more than ten years. When she began her teaching career in 1993, she faced many challenges. Chief among these was a lack of specialized training in Yup'ik reading/writing and appropriate classroom teaching methods. She writes in her application letter: "When I started teaching in the fall of 1993, I was not proficient in Yup'ik literacy. . . . I didn't know how I would teach reading and writing to the students. . . . I was fortunate to have Alice as a teacher-aide. She had tremendous knowledge in teaching Yup'ik, and had received training with the LKSD [Lower Kuskokwim School District] summer institutes. She taught me about Yup'ik vocabulary that I didn't know, and methods of teaching Yup'ik. She had tremendous knowledge to teach our language, and it refined my teaching techniques."

Like Moses, Oulton noted problems with students' grammatical accuracy. Using song, another type of story, she focused student attention on the form of the second-person genitive endings in Yup'ik. Students in her class learned songs and then composed their own songs with the structures under investigation. This second step pushed the students to produce output and create their own meanings through the language. Using a pretest/posttest design, Oulton found improvement in correct uses of the genitive endings that were targeted in the songs, but not in those that were not targeted (Oulton 2010).

When Sheila Wallace applied for the program, she was determined to develop a high school Yup'ik course for students who graduated from the K–6 immersion school in Bethel. These students had not had any Yup'ik language instruction since sixth grade and had begun to show signs of reduced proficiency and accuracy. This pattern reflected her own experience attending Bethel Regional High School years before:

> As a Senior . . . I took Yup'ik Language II offered at the school as an elective course. Being a speaker of Yup'ik, and being able to read and write it, I felt fortunate to have the option of expanding my Yup'ik literacy after a long absence from learning it in school. . . . Fortunately for me, the Yup'ik village that I grew up in [taught K–3 in Yup'ik]. When the opportunity to take Yup'ik as a language class became available to me at the Bethel Regional High School [BRHS], I . . . wanted to continue the learning path that gave me the sense of belonging and success [in elementary school]. As fluent Yup'ik speakers in kindergarten through third grade, we learned how to read, write, and speak Yup'ik which was a great comfort to many of us nervous village children entering the school system. Once I was in my high school Yup'ik class at BRHS, however, it became quite clear that the language class consisted of primarily non-Yup'ik speakers with the heavy emphasis on the arts and crafts instead of building language fluency and literacy. . . . I focused on my craft assignments in silence. I remember feeling that my ability to speak, read, and write in Yup'ik was largely ignored and devalued as I worked diligently on my Yup'ik crafts. Years later, when I returned to Bethel as a certified teacher I was not surprised to learn that Yup'ik for fluent speakers at BRHS was still not offered. (Wallace 2010)

The course Wallace developed was organized around types of storytelling: personal history; *yuuraq* (Eskimo dancing that tells stories); Yup'ik values, which tend to be imparted through storytelling; and Yup'ik fables.

To focus on developing oral proficiency, students used technology to create projects in the target language (Wallace 2010).

Theresa Prince was the elder for the cohort and the program. Although she did not earn her BEd until 2006, she worked first as a bilingual aide and then as a bilingual instructor beginning in 1971. In her letter of application, she writes: "At Kotlik Schools, I began working as a kindergarten aide back in the Bureau of Indian Affairs days. When Lower Yukon School District took over, I worked as a general aide and eventually became a bilingual instructor. In those times, I began taking college courses through audio-conferences. Finally and recently, I received my bachelors of education degree in May 2006. My supervisor thought it was a hard way to get a degree, but taking those courses in my own pace was a learning experience for me."

Today, the children of Kotlik grow up primarily speaking English. In her efforts to foster Yugtun development, Prince sought meaningful ways for elders to share their linguistic and cultural knowledge with her fourth-grade students, and she chose to investigate ways to make the elder's contribution comprehensible in the second-language classroom. To this end, she asked an elder to tell a story, once without providing props and then again with the assistance of images, props, and realia in an effort to make the story more comprehensible to the learners. She found that the second contextualized storytelling was indeed much more comprehensible to the students; they understood more elements of the story, paid attention longer, and enjoyed the story more. This project demonstrated how elders and teachers can work together to bring elder language and knowledge into the classroom through storytelling and comprehensible input. Because comprehensible input is the foundation for language acquisition, this represents an important first step toward richer learning opportunities for the learners in this context (Prince 2010).

Quana Holmberg is a kindergarten teacher in her hometown, a largely English-speaking village. Before she applied for the SLATE program, she attempted a master's in reading to better understand literacy acquisition among nonstandard English speakers and learners. In her application letter, she wrote: "I pretty much dropped the idea of getting my master's degree . . . until this SLATE opportunity came along! Now, I feel that I may have hope still. If I end up qualifying . . . I'd at least feel qualified to teach language effectively."

In her MA project, Holmberg used storytelling in a slightly different way. Conducting home visits to identify Yup'ik funds of knowledge and develop lesson plans based on these funds of knowledge, she asked parents to tell their stories. Her project is based on the stories told by the parents (Holmberg 2010).

MULTILITERACIES. Emily Vanderpool received her BAS in education from Western Oregon University in 2002 and began working in the Yup'ik region the following fall. She wrote in her letter of application: "I came to Alaska from Oregon after graduating college in 2002, and was looking for an adventurous place to start my teaching career. What I found was so much more exciting than I ever imagined. My first year in rural Alaska I found myself immersed in a new world, a new culture, and a new community of the warmest, kindest people I have ever met. . . . It didn't take long for me to realize that what had started as an adventure turned into a new lifestyle."

Vanderpool's primary objective in joining the SLATE program was to help her rural Alaskan students become fluent English readers and writers. She developed an approach combining the concept of literature circles[2] (Daniels 1994, 2001) with the new social networking and Web 2.0 learning tools, such as blogs and podcasts, that students use in their everyday lives (Vanderpool 2010).

Erin Kavanaugh received her BA in English and secondary education from the University of Wisconsin, Platteville, in 2003. She had been working in the Yup'ik region for two years when she joined the SLATE program. In her application letter, she wrote: "Since I have been employed with the Lower Kuskokwim School District I have become much more aware and involved in language work. I am currently teaching reading, writing and English Language Development to students in grades 6–12. All of my students have Limited English Proficiency status. Up until a year ago, my experience working with nonnative speakers of English was limited."

Kavanaugh's MA project developed a new type of writing instruction that combined writing workshop (Calkins 1994) and Six+1 Traits writing instruction approach[3] with Web 2.0 tools (Kavanaugh 2010).

Sally Samson is a K–1 teacher at Ayaprun Elitnaurvik Immersion School in Bethel. When she joined the SLATE program, she had been teaching at the immersion school for nine years. She explained that when she began teaching, she "knew nothing" about teaching Yugtun to English-only speakers, and she "knew nothing about five-year-olds and their learning habits." Her goal was to provide future teachers with materials that would help them so that they would "not start out like I did: lost and not knowing where to begin." Like all the teachers, before joining SLATE Samson often experimented in her classroom: "Ever since I started teaching in Yugtun, I've been experimenting with different teaching techniques in instructing students to read and write. . . . The results I'm finding so far is . . . that students that learn kinesthetically learn them quickly when the sounds are combined with movement. . . . I've always struggled with the assumption that the Yugtun alphabet was to be taught separately from Yugtun grammar and orthography just because that's how I learned them and that's how they are taught today" (letter of application).

Samson built on her own classroom experiments to develop a writing curriculum that incorporated *yuraq* (Yup'ik dance) to teach writing in Yugtun using the Six+1 Traits approach to kindergarten students. Her case study followed four emergent writers' development of their Yugtun writing skills through connections with similar processes described in the Six+1 Traits (e.g., word choice, organization, conventions) in learning *yuraq* (Samson 2010).

Sarah Bass has worked in a diverse set of educational settings both inside and outside Alaska. Immediately prior to returning to her home village of Hooper Bay as a kindergarten immersion teacher, Bass worked as an English-language development teacher in a Head Start program for immigrant children in Washington state. She explains her motivation for joining the SLATE program in her application letter: "The four years as an immersion teacher has been an experience of growth and appreciation for my language and culture. I want to continue working in maintaining the community's heritage language and culture. Living in the community and being involved with it, I have realized that what the students' needs are, as far as academics and growth. . . . My plan is to increase my knowledge in second language acquisition and development and learn methods that are and have been proven successful."

Bass's research documented the process of multiliteracies development of four kindergarten students. Her documentation included home literacy practices, such as drawing, Yup'ik storytelling, participating in subsistence activities (hunting, fishing, berry picking). Her data included parents' narratives and student work samples (e.g., student drawings and writing) as well as her own observations of student storytelling, singing, and chanting (Bass 2010).

When Mae Pitka joined the SLATE program, she was living her dream of teaching kindergarten and first grade in her hometown, Russian Mission. Pitka is an English-medium teacher, and although she is not a fluent Yup'ik speaker, she encourages her students "to use their language on a daily basis": "My goals and objectives are to give my primary students as much exposure to the literacy world and to appreciate language along with its role in their education. I know that language acquisition is an ongoing process and the more it is practiced, the better each child is in acquiring the skills necessary to communicate and read literature" (letter of application).

Pitka's research led to the development of a hands-on, multiliteracies learning center approach that incorporated culturally based stories and in- and out-of-classroom subsistence-based activities (e.g., berry picking, fishing) and field-based listening and drawing activities that took place in the village and on the river (e.g., sketch and sound journals) (Pitka 2010).

Joanne Sundown has a passion for multiculturalism. Before joining SLATE, she introduced the second-graders in her home village, Scammon Bay, to a diverse world: "This year I have begun to use [a thematic unit on diversity]. My overarching theme is that through the studies of all the continents and many different cultures of the world students begin to appreciate and value their own. I teach 2nd grade at Scammon Bay School. We have explored 6 out of 7 continents. Some of the countries we have studied include India, England, Brazil, Morocco, Egypt, Mali, and we are now beginning to study Australia" (letter of application). Building on her passion, Sundown developed thematic units using multicultural literature to explore how learning about other cultures could contribute to a deeper understanding and respect of one's own (Sundown 2010).

Cohort 2

Cohort 2, which consisted of teachers in the Assessment or Language Policy and Planning GRCs, included six Yup'ik and one non-Native MA/MEd candidate. Three were Yup'ik first-language speakers, two had relearned Yup'ik as adults, and two were monolingual English speakers. At the time, four were teaching through the medium of English, two were teaching Yup'ik in immersion schools, and one was employed as a Yup'ik specialist in her district's Office of Curriculum and Instruction.

- Six teachers are of Yup'ik descent.
- Three are Yup'ik first-language speakers; two relearned Yup'ik as adults.
- Age range: 29–53 years (mean 40.6, median 42).
- Three teach in English-medium schools; three teach in Yup'ik-medium schools; one is employed as a Yup'ik specialist in the District Office.

ASSESSMENT. As a Yup'ik education specialist, Rachel Nicholai frequently encounters people who blame Yup'ik programs for students' poor performance in school. In her experience, this blame game is intensified by the No Child Left Behind (NCLB)–mandated standardized tests as well as by outsiders to the language and culture pointing "teachers in different directions based on how they think Yup'ik children should learn" (Nicholai 2010, p. 2). These outsiders often see hands-on projects created in Yup'ik language and culture classes as just arts and crafts. "Often . . . mistakenly [assuming] that there is no link in learning [between] the product developed [and academic skills] . . . These assumptions can lead to blame games where administrators or teachers worry that students are 'left behind' in English and score below their grade level in their English standardized assessments. Because of this pressure, some Yup'ik programs in some villages have reduced their time frame for teaching Yup'ik language and culture" (Nicholai 2010, pp. 2–3).

In an effort to counter these stereotyped responses to Yup'ik language and culture programs, Nicholai (2010) focused her work on creation of authentic assessments for the Lower Kuskokwim School District's (LKSD) new *yuuyaraq* (the way of being a human) curriculum. In her work, she focused on exploring how Indigenous knowledge informs assessment within the Yupik region (Barnhardt & Kawagley 2005).

When Kristin Hendrickson joined the SLATE program, she was a new teacher living and working in a context completely different from any she had experienced before. She describes what this was like: "I have tried over and over again to describe this conflict in words that will help an outsider understand this dilemma, but I have concluded that the only way to truly understand it is to do what I have done. Only when I moved to a community that was so different (linguistically, geographically, etc.) from what I knew and was familiar with, got to know the people, their values, their history, and took time to listen and observe was I able to understand some things I could do to change the way I taught and assessed that expanded beyond the standards" (Hendrickson 2010, p. 2).

In her thesis, Hendrickson shares her successes, challenges, and discoveries while implementing authentic assessment, or meaningful multiple forms of assessment that reflect student learning, in her fifth-grade classroom. She describes the wealth of knowledge she gains about each learner when applying authentic assessments and contrasts that with insights gained from standardized tests alone. She also explores the tension she faces given the pressure the district and school face to meet annual yearly progress through standardized tests (Hendrickson 2010).

When Renee Green joined the SLATE program, she was working as a first/second-grade immersion teacher in the Yup'ik immersion program in her home village, Hooper Bay. Even though Green was not a fluent speaker of Yup'ik, she joined the Hooper Bay immersion program right after receiving her teacher certification in 2004, as she explained in her letter of application: "It is now 2007 and I have come a long way. For the early part of my career, I worked with three wonderful ladies who helped me to learn about my language and culture. In my first year, I worked with Juliana Springer and Laura Joseph (our aide). Together we cotaught 21 children. We did it in Yup'ik. The next year, I worked with Mary Anne Nukusuk and again with Laura Joseph. This time we worked with 26 children. Again we taught in Yup'ik. Those two years were the most challenging. Not only was I a teacher, I was also a learner."

Green's research drew on the knowledge and experiences of the Yup'ik teachers who taught in the immersion program at her school. Using focus groups, interviews, classroom observations, and field notes, her goal was to inform the whole school community about the needs of the Indigenous language program based on information from insiders in the community. The primary insiders included teachers who taught at the school. Many of these teachers described how continual assessments in English, rather than in Yup'ik, hindered the efforts of Yup'ik language revitalization programs. Because of NCLB, their students were required to take standardized tests in English based on curriculum focused on outside requirements. This push from the outside impacted many of the struggles teachers faced about language use in the classroom, assessment measures, and support for the program (Green 2010).

LANGUAGE POLICY AND PLANNING. When Anna Angiak-Bond joined the SLATE program, she had been working as an English-medium junior high/high school teacher in her home village, Tununak, for more than twenty years. As she explained in her letter of application, however, the techniques she learned to use did not always address the language needs of her students: "I have learned numerous techniques in teaching various content areas to Yup'ik students, or more appropriately, to 'ESL' kids. In retrospect, the techniques apply to cultural relevancy, but language? In reflecting as to why I should focus in the field of applied linguistics, I have come to the conclusion that a thorough understanding of language acquisition and myself as a Yup'ik speaker might help me to effectively enhance my teaching."

When Angiak-Bond applied for the SLATE program, she was unsure whether to focus on English or Yugtun. Soon after starting, however, she found her focus in questions of identity, language, and culture. She focused her thesis on her role as a mother working to reinvigorate Yup'ik for her preteen child, who had become English dominant and seemed to be on a path to language loss (Angiak-Bond 2010).

Atan (Veronica) Michael was an immersion teacher at Ayaprun Elitnaurvik when she applied for the SLATE program. In her application letter—the only letter written in Yugtun—she expressed her commitment to further her education for "the sake of our children, their parents, our elders and those who came before us." This commitment formed the foundation of her work and informed her investigation of the struggle she and two other mothers experienced in attempting to maintain Yup'ik in the home for their children (Michael 2010). In that investigation, Michael initially struggles with and ultimately reconciles the tensions she sees between the world her grandparents grew up in and the world her children will inherit. This same tension is evident in her letter of application.

> I remember one of our elders saying that we are not teaching our children Yup'ik ways of learning today; rather we are teaching the Western ways. But they [the elders] are just as proud to see our children [at Ayaprun] beginning to speak Yugtun. It is true what the elder had said: We literally translate what we [as teachers] see in English and provide the Yugtun translation for our students to learn . . . but I also realize that these elements that the children learn today albeit English are critical for the students' future and careers. . . . This also is in the forefront of my thoughts. Our Yup'ik ways has strength in the language; if we lose our language, we will lose our ways, as language is our strength. Since we rely so much on the Western ways . . . how can we move forward to strengthen our Yugtun ways of teaching?

Barbara Amos-Andrew teaches third grade in a K–3 immersion school in Kwethluk. Like many teachers in the program, she is deeply concerned about Yugtun language loss and sought out the SLATE program as a means to foster language revitalization: "These days, most children grow up speaking mostly English. Being an educator and teaching Yup'ik in our community would prolong our language to be used more on a daily basis. . . . As a Yup'ik speaker, [I want to] serve our people [by] being a role model to the younger generation, to parents . . . to district personnel, and to our region. . . . That way, our Yup'ik language will become stronger and [it will be] reinforced in more ways than one" (letter of application).

In her thesis, Amos-Andrew built on her desire to be a role model for local teens. She sought to understand the needs and goals of teenage girls in Kwethluk with a range of Yup'ik language abilities as her community experiences language shift (Amos-Andrew 2010).

When Jill Hoffman applied for the SLATE program, she had been an English-medium teacher in her hometown, Bethel, for more than ten years. After several years as a fourth-grade teacher, she decided to move to the lower grades "so that I could learn the process of reading from the earliest stages." Although she initially wanted to conduct research on reading development and the needs of limited English-proficient students, her son ultimately inspired a different research project: "I have a nine-year-old son who has been in Yup'ik Immersion since he started kindergarten. He is in fourth grade and can now speak Yup'ik fluently, which is quite amazing considering neither one of his parents can speak the Native language. It has been interesting to see the process of him acquiring the language . . . so I am getting a close view on the gaps that need to be filled. . . . This is the same struggle and concern that I have seen . . . from my students and parents" (letter of application).

Hoffman ultimately decided to explore the complex process of school choice for parents deciding between a Yup'ik immersion and an English-only school. Together these theses paint a complex picture of both language shift and the struggle to reestablish "local options, local control, local hope and local meaning to life" (Fishman 1991, p. 35) necessary for language revitalization to take hold (Hoffman 2010).

Physical Setting

All four classes took place in the summer session held in July 2008 on the campus of the University of Alaska Fairbanks. Cohort 1 was enrolled in Second Language Curriculum and Materials Development, cotaught by Sabine Siekmann (faculty member) and Hishinlai' "Kathy Sikorski" (Alaska Native PhD candidate), and Multiliteracies in Second Language Classrooms, cotaught by Joan Parker Webster (faculty member) and Theresa Arevgaq John (Alaska Native PhD candidate). Cohort 2 was enrolled in Assessment for the Second Language Classroom, cotaught by Marilee Coles-Ritchie (faculty member) and Walkie Charles (Alaska Native PhD candidate) and Language Policy and Planning, cotaught by Patrick E. Marlow (faculty member) and April G. L. Counceller (Alaska Native PhD candidate). Classes met four days a week (Monday, Tuesday, Thursday, and Friday). Wednesday and Saturday were designated as study and project days, respectively.

This is the backdrop against which we tell the story of the course planning, development, and specific learning activities that took place in these summer courses. We tell this story through events and conversations that occurred in the classes. However, the tale does not stop at the classroom door. It continues well beyond, spilling over into out-of-class times in which the teachers established collaborative relationships among themselves, deepened their knowledge and understandings, and established a true learning community that can only come with a joint commitment to preserving the Indigenous culture and language through sound teaching practices.

Notes

1. We adhere to the classification of dialects presented by Jacobson (1998). However, Krauss (1980) lists the following eight dialects: Bristol Bay, Coast, Hooper Bay–Chevak, Kuskokwim, Nelson Island, Nunivak, Yukon, and Igushik.

2. Literature circles are small, student-facilitated discussion groups in which individual students or partners take on roles and responsibilities for various elements (e.g., story summary, vocabulary, personal connections) of the text under discussion. For a detailed discussion of literature circles, see Chapter 4.

3. The Six+1 Traits approach to writing instruction was originally developed by Northwest Regional Educational Laboratory (now Education Northwest) and is based on the premise that good writing contains six basic traits: ideas/content, sentence fluency, organization, word choice, conventions, and voice. Presentation (how the text is presented on the page) was recently added to these original traits.

CHAPTER TWO

Mentoring

Engaging Communities of Practice

Joan Parker Webster and Sabine Siekmann

In Chapter 1, we provided an overview of the Graduate Research Collaboratives (GRCs) model, which was a primary organizational framework for students' research interests. Underscoring the concept of the GRCs was the goal of establishing relationships within a collaborative community of research and practice. In many graduate programs, faculty members are expected to engage in developing relationships with students to foster academic and professional growth. Typically, in the university context, mentoring is conceived of as a dyadic relationship that involves interaction between faculty and protégé-student. As with any relationship, interactions between people are framed by the social and cultural contexts and identities of the participants involved. In the university context, mentoring relationships are usually framed by the academic and organizational rules, norms, conventions, and practices (Chan 2008; Mullen 2005). But these interactions are also framed by cultural beliefs, values, norms, and protocols brought to the relationship by each participant. Although the academic focus often predominates in many faculty–student mentoring relationships, we knew that our approach had to bring together both the academic and cultural contexts to develop an effective mentoring component in the Second Language Acquisition Teacher Education (SLATE) program.

In this chapter, we discuss the development of our approach to mentoring. We begin with an overview of relevant literature on mentoring, which is organized into two broad topic areas: (1) mentoring functions, characteristics, and models; and (2) ethical issues. We then turn to our theoretical framework for mentoring and describe how we conceptualize our approach to mentoring and the evolution of our design for mentoring within the GRC model. Finally, we discuss the themes that emerged from debriefing sessions with doctoral students about their perspectives on what mentoring means in Indigenous contexts, as well as their reflections as mentors.

Overview of Relevant Literature

Mentoring Functions, Characteristics, and Models

In her seminal study on mentoring in the workplace, Kathy Kram (1985) identifies two primary mentoring functions: career-related functions (e.g., teaching, coaching, sponsorship, promoting visibility, advocating, and networking) and psychosocial functions (e.g., role modeling, acceptance and confirmation, counseling, and friendship). These functions can also apply in the university context. However, it could be argued that the most common functions of mentoring in the university context are those related to career development, and these are closely aligned with functions related to academic advising. According to Lewis Schlosser and Charles Gelso (2001), university faculty can be advisers and not mentors and mentors can mentor without advising. In any case, faculty and student mentoring relationships have increasingly been described as more reciprocal, mutual, and personal (Mullen, Cox, Boettcher, & Adoue 2000). This trend toward mutuality and advocacy on both personal and professional levels is evident in W. Brad Johnson's (2006) research, which identifies common components that characterize mentoring functions. These components include providing direct career assistance, serving as role models, developing enduring personal relationships, giving emotional support, and offering a safe environment for self-exploration. Johnson views mentoring as clearly distinct from other faculty roles, such as advising, such that the relationship is defined by intentional and developmentally generative career development.

The notion of mutuality is further developed in Johnson's (2008) rationale for a *transformational* model of mentorship, which is in contrast to a *transactional* model. In a transactional model, mentoring is more hierarchical and formal. The mentor performs certain functions, such as teaching, coaching, and advising; however, it is primarily a one-way, top-down relationship in which the mentor transmits knowledge to the passive protégé or mentee. Carol Mullen (2005) refers to this as technical mentoring, and Jennifer Walker (2006) calls it instrumental mentoring. In this kind of mentorship, the student is provided with resources when needed and given summative evaluations, but for the most part is left alone (Johnson 2008).

In contrast, transformational mentoring is more collaborative, reciprocal, and focused on partnering with protégés to help them through the developmental transitions in both graduate school and their professional careers (Johnson 2008). Mullen (2005) calls this kind of mentoring collaborative, and Walker (2006) calls it relationally oriented. Thus, transformational mentoring emphasizes mutuality and reciprocity in learning and also challenges the assumptions about hierarchy, academic rank, and status (Johnson 2008). According to Johnson, it is common for most faculty–protégé relationships to start in a transactional framework, which provides a structure in which the roles are clearly defined so as to reduce anxiety and unstability for the protégé. Then, as the relationship evolves and the protégé gradually becomes more confident in her role as a graduate student, academic scholar, and professional, there is greater movement toward a transformational model of mentoring.

Ethical Issues

TENSIONS IN MENTORING ROLES. Although greater collaboration, mutuality, and reciprocity in learning represent a positive shift for both mentor and protégé, there exists an ethical tension between these elements of good mentorship and the institutional gatekeeping requirement for evaluation of a protégé's competence and performance in her graduate studies. This duality of roles and duties can pose tensions for the mentor as well the protégé. According to Johnson (2008), multiple relationships (e.g., instructor, mentor, coach, advocate, colleague, friend) can "heighten the risk of conflicts of interest, exploitation of students, and diminished efficacy in the faculty role" (p. 38). Similarly, Lewis Schlosser and Pamela Foley (2008) identify potential ethical concerns that include issues of power, multiple and/or inappropriate relationships, boundary problems, and competence of the mentor.

As the multiplicity of roles increases for the mentor, a protégé's difficulty with handling the demands required by these roles can increase and cause incompatibility with her mentor. While the increase in collaboration, mutuality, and reciprocity in learning and the establishment of personal relationships may contribute to tensions in mentoring relationships, these elements have been identified as very important for women and students of color (Walker 2006). Therefore, it seems necessary to consider racial, social, and cultural perspectives when discussing ethical issues related to mentoring.

RACIAL, CULTURAL, AND SOCIAL ISSUES. There has been an increasing awareness of the importance of the role cultural diversity plays in understanding potential ethical issues in mentoring. According to Schlosser and Foley (2008), while ethical issues can emerge in all mentoring relationships, these issues can be influenced by the cultural identities of both mentors and mentees. For example, power differentials between faculty and students can exist in all mentoring relationships, and these can be intensified in relationships between mentors and students from disenfranchised cultural groups. Furthermore, Schlosser and Foley identify key cultural variables that can potentially affect faculty–student mentorships: race and ethnicity, age, gender and sexuality, religion, and ability status (e.g., visual, auditory, learning, or other impairment). All of these can be salient to cross-cultural mentoring relationships, and the most commonly cited issue and perhaps most salient to the SLATE program is the tension that can occur between relationships that include a white, European American faculty member and a student of color. However, the notion that only faculty of color can mentor students of color has been repudiated theoretically as well as empirically (Atkinson, Neville, & Casas 1991).

Another issue relevant to the SLATE program was the issue of age. Generally, the traditional image of a mentor is that she or he is older and therefore wiser with more experience. Thus, issues can emerge in relationships between mentors who are the same age as or significantly younger than their mentees. In these relationships, it can be easy for mentor and mentee to form close friendships and develop multiple relationships. However, tensions can arise when the mentor assumes the institutional role of evaluator (Schlosser & Foley 2008). It is also possible that in relationships in which mentors are much older than the mentee, the power differential increases so much that the mentee is not able to challenge the mentor's behavior, which can lead to exploitation of the mentee (e.g., using a student as research assistant without crediting or collaborating on academic publication or publishing student research as if it were one's own) (Schlosser & Foley 2008). In any case, it is critical to be conscious of the multiple identities of both mentors and students and the complexities of differences that make up these identities. It is also important for the mentor to recognize the potential tensions between individual and collective value and belief systems that can arise within the mentoring relationship as it progresses. By understanding the crucial role that both mentor's and the protégé's cultural identities play in a mentorship that emphasizes collaboration, mutuality, and reciprocity, the mentor can better attend to any ethical issues that emerge and meet the needs of the student as the relationship develops.

Building a Conceptual Framework for the GRCs

A primary consideration for building our conceptual framework for mentoring was how best to foster a truly collaborative and equitable conversation that would bring together the cultural perspectives and life experiences represented by all the stakeholders. Faced with a history of apprehension and mistrust by Indigenous communities for university-based researchers who privileged the established Western academic knowledge system, we sought to create a means for dialogue that was not based on hierarchical power relations and was more inclusive of Indigenous epistemologies and methodologies. Thus, it seemed imperative to situate our mentoring practice within a framework that supported a dialogue based in equity and trust between members of groups with such heterogeneous composition.

The Role of Intersubjectivity in Mentoring

Intersubjectivity has been defined as a process of communication in which those involved in a communicative event take the position of the other to come to a mutual understanding (Carspecken 1996; Habermas 1987). Intersubjectivity can also be applied to a learning event. In Lev Vygotsky's (1978, 1987) discussion of the Zone of Proximal Development (ZPD), intersubjectivity plays a key role. In Vygotskian terms, then, intersubjectivity is the process that occurs as participants, engaged in a learning activity or event, initiate a task with different understandings and arrive at a shared understanding as they collaborate. Thus, within the ZPD, an environment or context for guided or scaffolded participation is enacted such that learning can take place through intersubjectivity. As with Jürgen Habermas's (1987) notion of communicative action oriented toward understanding, the learning that takes place within the ZPD is based in social interaction and on the process of communication framed by the shared presuppositions of participants who are also engaged in intersubjectivity. Though the notion of intersubjectivity is paramount to communication and learning, the notion of shared presuppositions by the participants can often be a source of tension in a communicative/learning event, particularly when participants grounded in one cultural system are trying to function in another that is not culturally familiar or congruent. However, while this tension can be exacerbated by lack of sensitivity to other, nonmainstream cultural systems (as may occur in relationships involving Western academic researchers and Indigenous communities), it can play a role in challenging the status quo and lead to change in the participant or context. In other words, intersubjectivity in communication and learning seems to require a balance of shared presuppositions and differences in perspectives.

This role of tension seems related to Mary Louise Pratt's (1991) description of contact zones, which are defined as "social spaces where cultures meet, clash and grapple with each other, often in contexts of highly asymmetrical power" (p. 575). In her view, contact zones can be emotionally charged places where people can experience anger, hostility, and incomprehension. However, they can also be highly creative places where "moments of wonder and revelation, mutual understanding and new wisdom" (p. 586) can occur among the actors in the contact zone. If we consider contact zones as a space in which learning can occur, this bears a similarity to the Vygotskian notion of learning within the ZPD.

Building on this theoretical framework, we knew we could not create our concept of mentoring using the traditional Western academic model that suggested hierarchical, top-down, asymmetrical power relationships, because it seemed at odds with what we viewed as parallel concepts of communication oriented toward understanding and learning as it occurs within the ZPD. Therefore, we sought to build mentoring relationships that could be dialogic and reciprocal and involve multiple cultural resources working together to create ranges of potentials within ZPDs that emerge through group interaction. In our view, this could best be accomplished through the culturally congruent practice of collaborative activity, also referred to as joint activity (Rogoff 1990, 1993), which has also been described as a socially mediated process of coparticipation and colearning (Gutierrez, Baquedano-Lopez, Alvarez, & Chiu 1999).

Colearning through Joint Activity

Barbara Rogoff (1990), in developing her concepts of colearning through collaborative social activity, draws from the theories of Vygotsky (1978, 1987) and John Dewey (1916), which focus on children participating in joint sociocultural activity with other people in a social environment. Building on Vygotsky's notion of intersubjectivity, Rogoff (1990) suggests that the very notion of communication presumes intersubjectivity. Like Vygotsky, Rogoff views engagement in communication/intersubjectivity with other more knowledgeable members of the society, who are experienced with society's practices and use of tools (e.g., language) to mediate intellectual activity, as essential to children's cognitive development. Rogoff also builds on Dewey's understanding of the role that participation in joint activity with others within a social medium or context, with its accepted meanings, norms, and values, plays in the appropriation of the purpose, methods, and skills associated with the activity. In this way, the child or learner, by communicating intersubjectively verbally and nonverbally and doing her part in the joint activity within a sociocultural environment, bridges understanding between the known to the new, between one situation and another.

For Rogoff (1993), one cannot separate the relationship of individual development and social interaction from the cultural activity in which personal and interpersonal action takes place. Furthermore, the development of the individual cannot be viewed apart from the development of others involved, or even the cultural community itself. These interrelated relationships form the basis for inseparable concepts, which Rogoff calls apprenticeship, guided participation, and participatory appropriation, that reflect different planes of focus—community and institutional, interpersonal and personal—within sociocultural activity. These terms can be briefly described as follows.

- *Apprenticeship* extends the idea of apprenticing in a craft or trade (e.g., electrician, chef, graphic designer) to include participation in any other culturally organized activity, such as schooling, family relations, or community activities (e.g., subsistence hunting and gathering in some Indigenous communities). Apprenticeship reflects the community and institutional plane of focus.
- *Guided participation* refers to the processes that occur between people as they communicate and participate in culturally valued activity. Guidance involves the direction given by the participants in the social and cultural group (e.g., intersubjectivity) as well as cultural and social values and norms that underlie the direction or guidance given in the activity. Participation refers to observation as well as to hands-on involvement by participants within an activity. Guided participation reflects the interpersonal plane of focus.
- *Participatory appropriation* refers to the process of change that occurs in individuals as they appropriate what they learn from one activity to

> become prepared for involvement in other, similar activities. Participatory appropriation is a process of becoming rather than acquisition (e.g., dynamic rather than static) and reflects the intrapersonal plane of focus.

These notions of apprenticeship, guided participation and participatory appropriation put forth by Rogoff (1993) are not new to Yup'ik culture and the Yup'ik approach to teaching and learning. In research conducted in classrooms using Math in a Cultural Context (MCC), math modules based on Yup'ik cultural/subsistence activities,[1] Yup'ik teachers employed these notions as part of their instructional strategies. For example, when teaching students a lesson based in the cultural activity of creating geometric patterns (*tumuqcek*) for the border of a parka, Nancy Sharp (Lipka et al. 1995) brought in pieces from her mother's parkas to illustrate the connection to her own family and their distinctive family patterns. As she cut out pieces to create a pattern for a new border she was going to make, she told a story about how the border indicated family ties and how each family had its own distinctive pattern. This was in contrast to how many Western teachers demonstrate while giving step-by-step instructions. She gave students materials for the task and set them to work. Students naturally chose the groups they wanted to be in. In each of these groups, a more proficient student became the natural leader and others watched and followed along with their own work. Again, there was no step-by-step verbalization, only demonstration and participation. Some students remained at the table with Sharp and continued to observe. When these students were ready to go off on their own, they joined a group. All along, Sharp continued to do her own work and did not travel around the room to check on the students. If students needed help, needed clarification, or wanted to show their work to Sharp, they went to where she was working and she gave help, usually through demonstration. This kind of cocollaborative relationship, based in apprenticeship and joint productive activity, became a primary focus for our approach to mentoring.

Toward a Transformational Design for Mentoring

As described in Chapter 1, the GRC model was originally inspired by lab-based research. However, we soon discovered that our abstract construct when applied to mentoring changed as the program was implemented and all participants, including PhD and master's degree students, collaborated in turning theory into practice. Therefore, our theoretical framework for mentoring centered in intersubjectivity and joint collaborative activity was put into practice through interactions at all levels and through multidirectional dialogues.

Graduate school is difficult enough for traditional, full-time graduate students in an on-campus setting, where students have the opportunity to interact regularly with their adviser, committee, and peers. For distance students, establishing peer relationships can be especially difficult. Casual interaction between classes, in the office, or at the coffee shop is impossible. Yet these casual interactions are important for developing research ideas, exploring course material, and working through personal challenges associated with graduate school.

In the Alaskan context, distance students tend to be even more isolated. As a result, faculty may find it difficult to maintain contact with distance students, especially when students seem to "disappear"[2] for long periods. These "disappearing" students face enormous challenges. The extreme isolation of a small village, where access is limited to plane, boat, or snowmobile, creates a sense that "My village is my world" (Angiak-Bond 2010, p. 8), and close family connections both within and across villages mean that every community challenge, death, or medical emergency is a significant personal event.

As noted, the physical science lab provides an opportunity for more experienced graduate students to mentor newer students, in terms of the expectations of graduate school and the research field. In the GRC model, Alaska Native doctoral students were recruited as near-peer mentors in an explicit attempt to provide this sort of guidance. As in other cohort-based education, SLATE faculty further hoped that grouping candidates into smaller GRC cohorts would further help overcome the student isolation common in distance education.

As discussed in Chapter 1, the GRC model was inspired by the idea that streaming students into a set of cohorts based on identified needs in the context of Yup'ik and English language education would result in (1) rigorous research directly relevant to teachers, school districts, and communities; (2) high completion rates; and (3) timely degree completion. The goals of the model sought to encompass both transactional and transformative modes of mentoring.

Initial interactions between faculty members and both doctoral and master's degree students heavily focused on advising issues, such as registering for classes, filling out graduate study plans, and so on. Furthermore, particularly in the beginning of the program, it was largely and maybe necessarily the faculty members who defined the concept of the GRC model itself. Over time, the mentoring relationships between individual faculty members and their students evolved, and there was also a systemic change in the way the GRC model was conceptualized by the faculty.

Some of the changes on the conceptual level can be exemplified by the use of the dance fan metaphor that emerged in the fall 2007, after the first summer session. In preparing for a poster presentation at a national conference, the faculty were searching for a visual metaphor that would allow us to talk about the GRC model, preferably one that would signify the Yup'ik culture of the majority of our students. We chose the dance fan (see Figures 2.1 and 2.2) because it allowed us to represent the interrelated nature of the various stakeholders. Rather than being grounded in a typically Western hierarchical top-down model, the cyclical nature of this model allowed for more collaborative connections. The two circles representing the faculty member (inner circle) and doctoral student (outer circle) form the setting for and are connected to each other by the feathers, representing the group of master's students. In other words, the master's students are supported through both rings: the faculty member and the Indigenous PhD student. Both rings are necessary to create a stable foun-

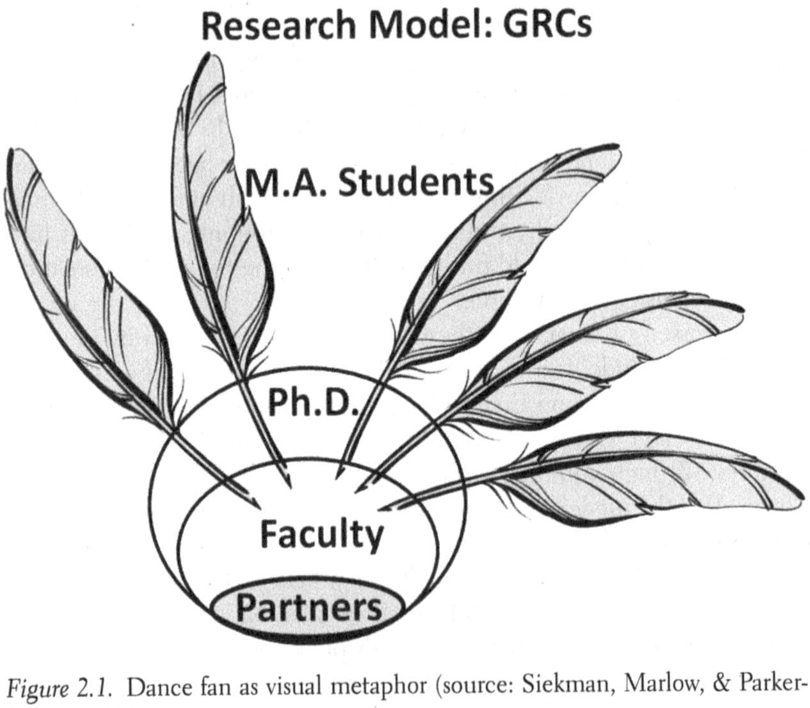

Figure 2.1. Dance fan as visual metaphor (source: Siekman, Marlow, & Parker-Webster 2008)

Figure 2.2. Men's dance fans used by student dance group at the University of Alaska Fairbanks (photo by W. Charles)

dation for the students. Finally, the binding of the grip indicates the important role we ascribe to the grant partners (local school districts and community organizations). Ultimately, the goal of creating community-driven research can be accomplished only through regular contact with representatives from the partners. In this view, then, the grant partners hold the entire structure together.

It should be noted that at its inception, the dance fan image was chosen primarily for its visual organization and its fit to the mentoring model developed in the original grant proposal. At that time, deeper epistemological considerations regarding the dance fan on a conceptual level or from the Yup'ik point of view had not been considered. However, according to Theresa Arevgaq John (personal communication 2011), the choice of the dance fan is highly symbolic because it reflects the deeper meaning of how dance pulls everyone together. In Yup'ik culture, music and dance are methods of bringing together stories from the whole world. Music and dance provide ways for people to collaboratively share and hand down cultural knowledge from generation to generation. Thus, choosing the dance fan to symbolize our goals for mentoring is both culturally appropriate and a highly significant representation of what we envisioned both conceptually and methodologically.

As faculty began to engage in more transformational modes of mentoring, particularly with our PhD students, we increasingly engaged in dialogue that was just as much a transformation for the faculty members as the students. In fact, particularly the doctoral students became mentors for us in terms of an Indigenous worldview. Students contributed knowledge about the cosmology, epistemology, and methodology unique to their own cultural group (e.g., Athabascan, Alutiiq, Yup'ik). In this way of sharing our individual stories through collaborative conversations, we came to understand the appropriateness of the dance fan metaphor on a conceptual level from the Indigenous point of view.

Methodology

In our search for a research methodology, we first determined that the primary goal of our study would be to focus on the concept of mentoring in cross-cultural contexts such as SLATE, as well as the processes guiding the development of mentorships. In keeping with our commitment to an Indigenous orientation to mentoring, the doctoral students' experiences as mentors and mentees became the focal point of our investigation into the mentoring process. Two inquiry points framed the study: (1) perceptions of what roles doctoral students played in mentoring and being mentored, and (2) the processes involved in how roles were defined and carried out in practice.

To explore these points, we first asked the doctoral students to each write a reflective vignette of their expectations and perceptions of their role as a mentor and how they carried out this role with the master's students in their respective GRCs. We provided three guiding questions to give them entry points for discussion.

1. What were your expectations for the SLATE model of mentoring in which doctoral students would mentor master's students in the GRCs as well as throughout the summer classes?
2. What did you view your role, responsibilities, and duties to be?
3. What were some specific instances that you recall of actual mentoring acts you have done over the course of the program as well as in the summers?

In addition, we met with the PhD students in a single two hour debriefing session on March 22, 2012 to engage in a conversation around their experiences of teaching and learning within their cultures and how this related to mentoring. The debriefing session was recorded and transcribed resulting in a 44 page transcript. The following questions guided this conversation.

1. How were you taught as children and young adults, and how is this idea of "mentoring" (or the significant word[s] describing the Yup'ik/Gwich'in/Alutiiq process) conceptualized and practiced in your cultures?
2. How did this fit (or not fit) with what you experienced in the Western notion of mentoring (as a student and as an instructor)?
3. How did both of these conceptualizations (Western experiences/Indigenous experiences) of mentoring influence your experiences with the SLATE master's students?

Our analysis of data is grounded in a constructivist grounded theory as put forth by Kathy Charmaz (2000). This approach requires a relationship with participants in which they can frame their stories in their own terms. Charmaz's version of grounded theory supports a cyclic process that allows the researcher multiple viewings of data. With each new viewing, initial ideas are expanded, new ideas are developed, and new questions to the data can result in coding and recoding data multiple times.

After an initial review of the data, we assigned preliminary codes. We then reviewed the codes and sorted them into categories. Table 2.1 provides an overview of these themes, subcategories, and modes of activity. These are each discussed in the following section.

Discussion of Themes

Roles

Roles are defined by unified modes of activity that can be recognized and practiced by those within the cultural group. Unlike static, norm-based roles assigned to participants in educational settings like faculty, mentor, chairperson, and so on, we view roles as based in communicative interaction and activity. Furthermore, interactions and activity are shaped by the cultural context in which they take place. Thus, roles can evolve and change.

Table 2.1. Mentoring Themes, Subcategories, and Activity Modes

Themes	*Subcategories*	*Mode of Activity*
I. Roles Unified modes of activity recognized and practiced by actors within a cultural context	Teacher-Learner	Storytelling: use of Indigenous method to inform and instruct Listening and observing: use of Indigenous method of learning through silent observation Demonstrating and modeling: Indigenous method of teaching and passing down cultural knowledge through active demonstration of task, usually without verbal explication typical of Western instructional methods
	Culture Bearer	Passing down cultural knowledge through the practice of cultural activities; based in first-hand experience of living within the culture
	Heritage Language Advocate	Uses heritage language in informal conversation outside class setting and as language of instruction in class activities
II. Relationships Within each role, a range of relationships developed, influenced by factors such as age, emotional needs, and so on	Educational-academic needs	Counsels and advises on topics related to academic theories and practices and provides expertise and help with class assignments
	Age	Counsels and advises based on years of experience and acquired expertise; is viewed by participants as cultural elder; also receives cultural guidance from cultural elders in cohort
	Gender	Counsels and advises in terms of familial/social structures—aunt, uncle, male hunter, female gatherer, female elder, and so on
	Interests	Develops friendships based on common interests
	Personal/emotional needs	Counsels, advises, develops friendships and offers assistance based on teachers' personal and emotional needs

The first theme emerging from the data involved the roles of Teacher-Learner, Culture Bearer, and Heritage Language Advocate, enacted by the PhD students through interactions and activity (see Table 2.1). The various roles emerging from our analyses are interrelated, and they are also distinct because of the particular mode of activity foregrounded in the performance of that role. For example, the role of Culture Bearer was enacted through the activity of imparting cultural knowledge. This cultural knowledge was sometimes relayed through the heritage language, and the role of Heritage Language Advocate was also enacted. However, because the primary purpose of the interaction and mode of activity was imparting cultural knowledge, the role of Culture Bearer is foregrounded. The following section presents each role as described by the PhD students.

TEACHER-LEARNER. John describes the concept of being a Teacher-Learner in terms of growing up in a community that adhered to traditional Yup'ik values and practiced culturally based subsistence activities.

> In terms of material learning when we sew something and there's a little part where it's crooked we had to undo the whole thing and resew it again and it's because our educators—they're our moms, aunts or grandmothers—want us to improve in what we're doing. I remember having to undo ten inches of fur sewing and I go, "Oh, no then I have to redo it again" and they said "You have to learn; you have to become patient and you have to know when things are good and when things are bad." And they say you will become lazy and you will be labeled as that type of worker or creator of something if you don't improve your work and they never told us "that is very good"; they always said "next time you will do a little bit better, next time it will become better." So in a way it is like an inspirational tool for us to say "I've met the standards thus far and yet I could become an even better sewer, a better oral storyteller, a better dancer, a better caretaker of my siblings." (debriefing session)

In this statement describing the cultural practice of skin sewing, John references the three modes of activity that characterize the Teacher-Learner Role: storytelling, listening and observing, and demonstrating and modeling. For example, in her description of how her teachers—mothers, aunts, grandmothers—"instruct," we see that it is through story about how to be a good person, which is necessary to becoming a good skin sewer. Though tacitly implied, listening and observing is the mode of activity that is partnered with storytelling in instruction. In other words, John implies that silently listening and observing was part of the learning process that occurred while her teachers were demonstrating and modeling how to sew.

In the following sections we provide more in-depth discussion about these interrelated and complimentary processes that support a theoretical and practical approach to an Indigenous pedagogy, using the words of the doctoral students.

STORYTELLING. Storytelling is central to many Indigenous cultures' discourse. In other words, it is a mode of activity that can be called a genre, but in Indigenous cultures, it is more a way of communicating. In the data, the participants describe storytelling in two ways—how it operates as discourse, and how it is used as a teaching tool.

In the following example, April G. L. Counceller describes storytelling as a practice that is implicitly understood as a method of imparting knowledge. In other words, when one tells a story, it is not announced or related in a step-by-step process: "Now I am going to tell a story about how to . . ." Rather, the story is related as the activity is being demonstrated: "There wasn't often a real overt 'this is learning time' or explaining what's going on. It was more like 'come help me fix the net' and my dad would just be fixing it and I'd be holding it and I wouldn't necessarily be thinking at the time 'I am learning this' I was just sort of there. . . . I would do things with the family like go and check the crab pots, and never was anything ever explained, 'this is what I was doing; this is why we're putting the crab pots here,' it was just lived experience" (debriefing session).

Walkie Charles gives an explicit example of storytelling as a teaching tool. In his retelling of being disciplined as a child, he recounts how his father used a story as an indirect way of instructing him on the correct way to act: "If I had done something wrong or if I had misbehaved during the day my father would not reprimand me immediately, but he'd be watching and when things were calm and we were all settled at home together my dad would tell a story about a little boy who might have done something similar. As a child I remember thinking, 'I know why he's telling this story, it has something to do with what I didn't do right today,' so indirectly in a story I was reprimanded" (debriefing session).

The notion of storytelling as discourse and using this technique as a teaching tool is also illustrated when Charles talks about his own teaching practice as a university instructor. "The way that I teach best is if I can connect myself to the way that I was taught. . . . I really like what Theresa said earlier about scaffolding. Basically what she was saying is you try something and if it doesn't work, then you strip it and you redo it and try again. And that is why I use that in my classroom today, '*Asirrpa* [that's good], let's try it again'" (debriefing session).

LISTENING AND OBSERVING. The activity mode of listening and observing is the compliment to the verbal method of storytelling and the physical method of demonstrating/modeling, which is described shortly. In the Indigenous approach to teaching and learning, paying attention and being actively engaged in learning is not necessarily exhibited by questions and answers, back-channeling, maintaining eye contact, and so forth, but more often through quiet observation and listening. This involves a focus of mind and body. Charles talks about the importance of listening and observing as the compliments to storytelling in remembering his father's philosophy of learning and teaching: "The quote that I refer to of my father many, many times . . . 'when we take the opportunity to listen and we take the opportunity to observe then we too might have a story to tell'" (debriefing session). He goes on to describe how listening and observing are interpreted as passivity and nonengagement by some teachers, particularly non-Indigenous teachers in Western educational settings. "As we were growing up listening and observing was one of the biggest things that we had to do. And that's why some teachers would say 'Wow those little Yup'ik kids are so quiet.' Well, that is because they're listening and they're observing before they say anything. And, during the time that I might be asking questions, something that I might have learned or should have learned might have passed. And so it was critical for me growing up to observe and listen. That is how I was taught" (debriefing session).

Hishinlai' "Kathy R. Sikorski," in talking about the importance of learning through observation, makes the connection to subsistence activities: "It's (learning) probably by observing and you don't even know you're learning those things. . . . Paying attention to where you are going, and there're things that you learn but, you don't realize that you are learning it. We always lived off the land. So, for instance, when you walk on the land, you can't just stomp around and make a lot of noise" (debriefing session).

MODELING AND DEMONSTRATING THROUGH HANDS-ON ACTIVITY. The activity mode of modeling and demonstrating is the physical method of teaching and learning. The Yup'ik notion of modeling and demonstrating is expressed as a joint activity that occurs side by side rather than face to face. John describes how her grandmother taught her dancing, sitting on her lap at an early age: "I remember my arms being held by an adult, by my grandmother apparently. She was singing songs and I was sitting on her lap and I was taught all these gestures to these songs. I didn't even know what they meant. And so by the time I was able to stand up and walk I already knew exactly what to do. So, with that kind of upbringing, we imitate our parents' teachings so we're using our hands all the time. . . . That's the modeling we are taught . . . so we learn to conceptualize through the music and then through hearing stories" (debriefing session).

This is quite different from the Western notion of instruction through modeling, which usually involves the teacher facing the students as she or he demonstrates a skill or task. In the Indigenous approach, described by the PhD students, the teacher and learners participate alongside one another. The key difference is rather than observing a mirror image, the image is parallel. Implicit in this methodology is that physical barriers, such as a lectern or table situated between the teacher and learner, are removed, and a more collaborative relationship is created. Charles describes it in this way:

> When sitting side by side the teacher uses his right hand, the student uses her right hand; and if the teacher uses his left hand the student uses her left hand. The idea is, I'm gonna learn something more because there's no barrier between us; and then if I sit across from somebody I feel that even though it's not a barrier there's something physical between us to where I might hesitate in responding or joining or sharing or talking. That's just one of the elements about how I was taught as a child and then as a young adult; of course things change because I went to boarding school and I had to learn to talk across tables, across barriers; and I realized in doing that I had to raise my voice to be heard from the other side. Whereas when you sit side by side, you can speak quietly and say things so that we could both understand and let our breaths out at the same pace. But if I talk to you across from the other side I'm gonna have to raise my voice so that you could hear me. (debriefing sessin)

CULTURE BEARER. The role of Culture Bearer is performed by the activity mode of passing down cultural knowledge through the practice of cultural activities based in firsthand experience of living within the culture. The essence of this role is captured by John's description of what it means to live the Yup'ik way and the responsibility of passing down cultural knowledge to future generations: "I remember my grandmother always told us, when you wake up in the morning think about how you're going to be using your whole day, how you're going to treat your siblings and your peer group and at the end of the night remember to analyze how you lived and if there're some things you want to fix think about those things and in future you won't repeat those again" (debriefing session).

John expresses this philosophy in an explicit goal associated with her role as an Indigenous near-peer mentor to SLATE master's students: "My role was to enhance Indigenous conceptual theories and methodologies and bring these into discussions about developing culturally based curriculum" (vignette). Similarly, Charles viewed his role as a "Yup'ik male" that brought with it the cultural meaning of being a "provider." For him, this carried the responsibility of "maintaining the heritage language and culture for Alaska's future generations" (vignette).

John and Charles often prepared Yup'ik food for students so they could feel a connection to the village even though they were in a very different and perhaps strange environment of the university and Fairbanks. Charles states: "During the second summer, I thought it would be a good idea to provide the master's students some Yup'ik soul food. Since we had an hour and a half lunch time, I prepared traditional dishes and invited everyone over to one of the classrooms on campus. It was good for all of us to share *neqpaq* [real food] as a group" (vignette).

Similarly, John prepared Yup'ik food and invited students over to her house, which provided them a space—one not bound by academic expectations—that was a free zone that could be framed by them in their Native language. She describes these times this way: "I often invited students to my home to enjoy Native food, speak Yugtun. It was a cultural space, but we could also discuss and brainstorm research concepts and methodologies in a comfortable, safe, nonacademic environment" (vignette).

For Sikorski, the notion of being a culture bearer by providing an Indigenous perspective carried some anxiety. She states:

> I must say that I was quite nervous about being the only Gwich'in Athabascan amongst the mostly Yupik Eskimo group. I wasn't sure how I should behave because as a Gwich'in person, I have a loud laugh, speak my mind, am proud of my culture, and am assertive. I've observed Yup'iks in other situations as being calm, quiet, and gentle, but also eating strong-flavored foods that do not agree with my diet. I was confused about how to behave amongst them. As it turned out, it seemed the reaction about cultures was reciprocal. We shared many of the same cultural traits . . . humor, laughter, respect, kindness, etc. As a result, I became friends with some of those with whom I had close contact. (vignette)

HERITAGE LANGUAGE ADVOCATE. The role of Heritage Language Advocate is enacted through the activity mode of using the heritage language (Yugtun) in informal conversation outside of the academic setting and as the language of instruction in class activities. Because the majority of master's students were Yup'ik and many also spoke Yugtun, the two Yup'ik doctoral students (Charles and John) found that their mentoring tasks included helping students with the dialogue between concepts as described in Yugtun and as described in English. Because of their backgrounds in both languages and also in Indigenous and Western academic discourses, they were able to mediate the master's students' understandings in this regard.

John explains how the use of Yup'ik facilitated deeper engagement and understandings for the master's students. In her case, these conversations largely occurred informally outside of class, such as those described under the Culture Bearer role:

> Part of my role I remember was translating and interpreting for them what they can't understand in Western language into Yugtun so they can start processing that. Having that relationship helped them to say, "Okay I can do it then. Okay, then I can talk to my professors. I know now what this means in Yugtun. Now I get it." And that level of being able to come to us and say "Arevgaq, what does this mean, I don't understand? What do linguists mean by this concept?", so I would to the best of my ability say it in Yugtun. In Yugtun way, here is how we could deal with that. So the freedom of them to come to me and then to Walkie, too, for further understanding or better understanding was one of those processes that they took advantage of. And they felt comfortable that they could rely on us. I think having that ability to have open conversations all the time strengthened that opportunity so that there can be ongoing dialogue. [It] is a healthy process for them to say, "Yes, we have our language to use. We have dual languages to deal with." (debriefing session)

Charles focuses more on the use of the heritage language within the classroom. He writes: "It became quickly apparent that the master's students spoke Yugtun freely during class. It seemed that whenever the students came across a concept that they felt would better be explained in Yugtun rather than in English, one student would begin speaking Yugtun and the others would follow. Seeing that happen, I began to use Yugtun at times during class instruction and in small groups" (vignette).

The ability to use Yugtun in their graduate studies had a powerful impact on the master's students, as exemplified by the following story, relayed by Charles: "I told the students, for this quiz use the language of your choice to express the topics that we've covered this week and [Name] was writing and while she was taking the quiz she started crying and I thought maybe she was having difficulty. I went up to her and I said, [Name] 'Are you okay?' in Yup'ik. And she said 'I'm fine. This is the first time that I've ever had to take a graduate course in my life where I could write in Yup'ik because I have a professor who is able to read and understand it. That's why I'm crying.'" (debriefing session).

Recognizing the importance of providing heritage language support created some difficulty for the doctoral students, Sikorski and Counceller, who were not Yup'ik and did not speak the language. For example, Sikorski explains: "Well, I think I have a totally different experience because when I started I didn't understand Yup'ik, I didn't know the culture and I think I felt like being cautious because I didn't want to say something or do something that would make the students feel like I was trying to show no respect" (debriefing session).

The difficulties perceived by Sikorski and Counceller were mediated by a feeling of solidarity with the other students in being Indigenous, which ultimately transcended language and cultural barriers. As the SLATE program developed, all students—both master and doctoral—were further unified through their common-held beliefs in eradicating and replacing hegemonic colonizing practices, particularly in relation to language revitalization and maintenance and education. Therefore, although the roles were sometimes discussed in more Yup'ik cultural terms, they were at the same time framed by the commonly held understanding of Indigenous modes of activity, and this resulted in a unified approach to enacting and communicating through those roles.

Relationships

A natural outcome of performance of roles through interactions and activity is the development of relationships. In this section we discuss the relationship theme, which is influenced by factors such as educational/academic needs, age, gender, interests, and personal/emotional needs. The theme of relationships is always present within the roles as described in the first theme.

In reflecting on his experience as a SLATE doctoral student and near-peer mentor, Charles poignantly makes the analogy to family: "If I had to do SLATE over again, I would, because this is home; this is family; this is what the support is. I have a new family and a family for life" (debriefing session). This kind of support helped doctoral students and master's students establish personal relationships. These personal relationships seemed to contribute not only to their individual growth academically but also to creating and nurturing a community of learners involving all of the SLATE participants. As Indigenous PhD students, Charles, Counceller, John, and Sikorski had a shared sense of purpose with the master's students. However, as John explains, ultimately relationships were defined not by credentials and job titles but by personal connections: "Knowing that there were such commonalities and similarities and that level of respect for each other as faculty, friends, sisters, and colleagues really brought peace and harmony to the environment in my opinion. We treat each other as human; not as 'she's a faculty, I'm a student and they are master students.' It was a community of learning. Our students were nontraditional. They were professionals themselves, and I think that fact that we all had that collaborative knowledge and that effort made it a positive experience and a successful one" (debriefing session).

Furthermore, similarities were not simply defined through a shared cultural background. Sikorski, a Gwich'in Athabascan, also found ways to connect to the master's students in individual and personal ways. She writes: "Small things that seemed mundane helped me to connect with the SLATE master's students. I tried to get to know some of them. I was going to the gym at the time and that's where I met some of the people that worked out and I got to know them a little bit. And then [Name]'s humor is just exuding from her so I immediately knew that's my way in with her. And then of course there're people who are very serious too. Like [Name] is very serious about her work and so I can have that side, too. And then I also had the research experience" (vignette).

Counceller, the PhD student with the least direct university teaching experience, summarizes her experience: "I do feel like the community that we created was really the thing that kept me in the program; that sort of family that we created. The mentorship model and the other Native students really helped bring the Indigenous aspect into it for me. But also being forced to survive in that Western context and providing the support that was needed also showed me what I might need to do for my Native students that I'm working with in the new Alutiiq studies program" (debriefing session).

Concluding Thoughts

Where do we go from here? It is probably expected that we construct a list of things that worked for us and things we found challenging and suggest a step-by-step plan for how to develop a mentoring program for similar settings. While these conclusions might help us reflect on our story about mentoring in the SLATE context, it would fit only our story. Telling our story as we have might help others think about their stories in relation to ours. However, our story cannot be someone else's story. The processes we engaged in are grounded in an understanding that the ways mentoring roles and relationships develop are dependent on and influenced by the physical and sociocultural context and the social and cultural identities of those involved in the relationship; thus, the notion of developing a step-by-step recipe for success seems antithetical. Because we have been a part of a dynamic learning process, we have come to a deeper understanding and belief in a sociocultural approach to learning based in intersubjectivity that cannot be described in terms of a static, one-size-fits-all process. Rather, the process always looks different because the learning that takes place in the ZPD involves ranges of potentials and engages multiple zones of proximal development. We view mentoring as a process that is like the learning as it happens in the ZPD, so mentoring can also be seen as a creative activity that is not *about* a topic or task—not a rote memorization of facts or enacting of set procedures. Instead, mentoring is a process in which we negotiate meaning together through our ever-changing roles of teacher and learner.

Now you may be thinking that this seems reasonable, but this is a Western perspective developed by a Western theoretician. True, but as we have attempted to illustrate, this notion of learning as a joint, collaborative activity is also a key element in an Indigenous, Yup'ik approach to teaching, learning, and mentoring. Perhaps this idea of bringing together Indigenous and Western epistemologies and methodologies into a third space is the key take-away understanding that seems unique to our story. Time after time, in enacting of roles and forming relationships, the students and faculty in the SLATE program found themselves working together to negotiate common ground and develop new understandings within this third space. Yet even though this space was, as Pratt (1991) describes, sometimes filled with anxiety and incomprehension, it was also a space for creativity where new knowledge and new relationships were forged.

For those of us involved in the SLATE program, the idea of reframing mentoring and building a community of practice, both born in a third space, was an exciting process. But it can also be a scary one. The practice of bringing together Indigenous and Western theories and methods into a third space can be highly contentious and anxiety-producing in many academic contexts. We have learned that if you can use that tension as a catalyst for learning and are open to scaffolding by others, you can build on existing knowledge and also create new and deeper understandings, create new possibilities, and tell your own stories.

Notes

1. MCC is a supplemental elementary school math series resulting from a university–school–community collaboration. This collaboration spans nearly two decades of work: forming meaningful relationships between the parties of this work produced culturally relevant materials that connect local knowledge to school knowledge and include integrated materials (literacy, geography, and science). Rigorous experimental and quasi-experimental designs in numerous studies found MCC to be effective (Math in a Cultural Context n.d.).

2. Among University of Alaska Fairbanks's Education faculty, a distance student is said to "disappear" when they skip one or more semesters of enrollment, often without notifying their adviser or other faculty or staff. The sense that the student has simply disappeared is reinforced by the fact that distance students may have little or no casual face-to-face contact, thereby requiring faculty and staff to take an active role in reinstating contact with them.

CHAPTER THREE

Reinventing Technology

Computers as Tools for Coconstructing the Local Voice in Materials Development

Sabine Siekmann and Hishinlai' "Kathy R. Sikorski"

This chapter is based on data collected as part of a larger, longitudinal study of the Second Language Acquisition Teacher Education (SLATE) project. Specifically, we report on data collected during a Second Language Curriculum and Materials Development course held in summer 2007. The course as a whole was undergirded by a constructivist, project-based methodology drawing on sociocultural theory (SCT). The course had two primary goals. During the first half, we aimed to engage the teachers in critical reflection on curriculum development in their own teaching contexts. In the second half, we focused largely on the uses of technology in developing and sharing culturally appropriate materials. We wanted to engage the teachers in critical reflection on the role materials and e-materials play in the language learning classroom, while at the same time integrating hands-on project-based learning through the creation of technology-enhanced materials for their classrooms. The question to what extent computer technology is appropriate for the teaching of Yugtun to elementary-age students in rural Alaska was a key point of discussion and will be explored in this chapter. Consequently, the focus here will be on the computer-assisted language learning (CALL) component of the course, the second half of the class, comprising four content days, three project days, and one day for presentations.

The chapter is organized into four main sections. After an introduction, we describe our framework, including a rationale for teaching CALL as part of the SLATE curriculum, the course goals and content, as well as our teaching methodology. The majority of the chapter is dedicated to a discussion of two themes that arose from the data: (1) initial resistance to using technology, and (2) making technology Yup'ik. We conclude with a summary of lessons learned and a description of next steps.

Before going into more depth about the themes emerging from this course, we want to bring attention to some important aspects in which our class differed from the others discussed in this book. The three other courses were foundational for a specific Graduate Research Collaborative (GRC) group (i.e., teachers in the assessment GRC enrolled in the Assessment course, etc.). However, all the teachers had taken the course "Theory and Methods of Second Language Teaching" during the previous semester. Therefore, the curriculum and materials development course, though potentially relevant to the teachers in the pedagogies GRC, did not relate directly to the teachers' thesis/project topics in the same way. Furthermore, because Hishinlai' was under time pressures to complete her master's thesis, this course did not evolve out of an independent study with the PhD student. In addition, although Hishinlai' had extensive experience in curriculum and materials development, neither materials development nor technology was a primary interest in her thesis or dissertation. As a consequence, the faculty advisor (Siekmann) did the primary planning for the course. The faculty member and doctoral student only had one joint planning session leading into the course. One final significant difference between this course and others reported on here is that although the Indigenous master's students are all Yup'ik Eskimo, and the other PhD students are either Yup'ik Eskimo or Alutiiq Eskimo, Hishinlai' is Gwich'in Athabascan. We now describe our framework for the course in more detail before discussing the themes emerging from the course implementation.

Framework

This section provides the rationale for teaching Indigenous language teachers about applications of technology in language learning and describes the theoretical foundation for the course goals and content as well as the teaching methodology.

A Rationale for CALL

Research in CALL, here broadly defined as uses of computer technology to assist the teaching and learning of second or foreign languages, originates primarily in the teaching of world languages and English as a second language (ESL). In this section we outline some of the key potential benefits ascribed to CALL and establish links to the specific needs of Indigenous language teachers and learners. This will serve as a rationale for why we included a CALL component for this particular group of teachers.

CALL has shown benefits to language learning in a variety of ways. It is beyond the scope of this chapter to review the field as a whole; please refer to Arnold and Ducate (2011), Belz and Thorne (2006), Chapelle (2001), and Fotos and Browne (2004) for more complete reviews. Here we focus on two topics directly linked to the needs of students learning Yugtun: access to authentic language, and increased opportunities for target language output and focus on form.

Access to Authentic Language

For world languages, websites provide virtually unlimited access to authentic language materials, that is, those prepared by native speakers of the language for native speakers of the language. Two key benefits proposed for authentic materials are that (1) they offer opportunities to listen to and read the target language produced by a broad range of speakers/writers in terms of age, gender, and regional dialect; and (2) they provide insights into authentic cultural content. Target language websites provide access to up-to-date culturally relevant information, allowing students to take virtual field trips to an environment where the target language is used. Through these field trips, students are able to see what speakers of that language are interested in and talk about and how they "see the world."

The full range of dialects, worldviews, and cultural information can never be imparted by one teacher or native speaker. Therefore, the Internet becomes an important tool to engage with the target language and culture. In Indigenous language learning contexts, access to different dialects and elders who can impart the most sophisticated linguistics forms and provide access to invaluable cultural information is of great importance. Not every Indigenous language teacher has advanced levels of language proficiency and generally will not feel comfortable claiming expertise in all aspects of culture. Therefore, participation by elders (who represent the native speakers from the world language education perspective) is very desirable, but not always possible. Internet resources could make linguistic and cultural information more widely accessible to teachers and learners. However, although world language teachers have a virtually unlimited supply of easily accessible web pages at their fingertips, the same is not true for teachers of Indigenous languages. For example, there is no Yugtun version of Google, and a Google search for "Yup'ik" results in pages *about* Yup'ik culture and language but not *in* Yugtun. In the case of Yup'ik, large collections of oral and visual materials are archived, for example, at the Alaska Native Language Center, but teachers cannot easily avail themselves of these resources because they are not accessible online (as of this writing). Also worth noting is that the nature of these resources is fundamentally different from typical online resources. The archives include both published (grammar books, dictionaries, word lists, school books, elder narratives, etc.) and unpublished (research notes, grammatical descriptions, word lists, interview transcripts) materials, as well as original video and audio recordings of interviews and public events. In short, except for the published material, the rest is largely unprocessed data. A web page is, in essence, always processed. Few (if any) web pages have been created in Yugtun, created by Yup'ik people for Yup'ik people.[1] Consequently, one goal of the class was to enable teachers to create Yup'ik language websites for use by students, teachers, and community members.

Increased Opportunity for Target Language Output and Focus on Form

Merrill Swain (1985, 2000) has argued that language learners need more than comprehensible input (as offered, for example, through authentic language materials) to reach higher levels of language proficiency. She argues that producing output in meaningful situations allows learners to "notice the gap" between what they can already do and what they are trying to express. It helps learners focus on both the meaning and the form at the same time, leading to higher levels of accuracy. In this view, speaking and writing in the target language is critically important for language development. Through language output, learners realize how their own language production differs from that of a native speaker and might not be comprehensible to their interlocutors; in other words, they notice the gap between what they wish to say and what they are able to say. Producing language to communicate further enables learners to test their hypotheses—to gather invaluable information about whether their assumptions about how the target language works are correct. In these ways, output allows learners to reflect on their language use. In this view, speaking and writing are not the outcome of language learning, as proposed by Stephen Krashen (1981). Instead, speaking and writing in meaningful contexts is a necessary part of the language learning process (Swain 1985).

Computer-mediated communication (CMC) offers ample opportunities for learners to produce output and interact with speakers and other learners of the target language in meaningful contexts. Person-to-person, small-group, or whole-class conversations can be set up through asynchronous tools such as email, blogs, or discussion boards or through synchronous tools such as chats, instant messaging, or voice over Internet protocol (VOIP) applications such as Skype. For example, through key-pal programs or tandem-learning experiences, students learn the language and engage in intercultural exchanges (Thorne 2006). In the Yup'ik context, CMC would take place most likely between learners of Yugtun who live in different villages. Because villages differ considerably not only in dialect but also in terms of cultural practices, learners can engage in meaningful explorations of both language and culture within the context of the same language. One of the main benefits of CMC is that when communicating with other learners (within their own classroom or with learners elsewhere), the number of "channels" available in the classroom are multiplied, providing opportunities for several conversations to occur at the same time, thereby increasing the amount of output produced by each student. Rather than answering questions posed by the teacher one by one, students engaged in email, chat, or VOIP exchanges pose and answer questions in pairs or groups. In this way, each student produces and processes more language in the same time period. Furthermore, learners have more opportunities to ask their own questions, thereby creating a more student-centered learning environment.

Most of the teachers taking the curriculum and materials development class were teaching either in Yup'ik-medium schools or were teaching Yup'ik language classes. All were rural teachers in isolated villages who wanted to improve the language proficiency of their students in either English or Yup'ik. Thus, the rationale for introducing CMC tools (blogs, Skype, and wikis) was to enable their students to establish meaningful interactions with other learners, providing increased opportunities and requirements for output.

Through engaging learners in meaningful interaction, CMC exchanges can also serve as starting points for more form-focused activities. Michael H. Long (1991) defines focus on form: "Whereas the content of lessons with a focus on forms is the forms themselves, a syllabus with a focus on form teaches something else [content] . . . and overtly draws students' attention to linguistic elements as they arise incidentally in lessons whose overriding focus is on meaning, or communication" (p. 46). Focusing on accuracy in otherwise meaning-focused interchanges, such as through CMC, has the potential to improve accuracy of learner utterances, which is a major concern in the region, especially in the Yup'ik-medium schools. Scholars involved in research in immersion settings (see, for example, Genesee 1987; Lazaruk 2007; Swain 1985) have demonstrated that learners in these environments develop high levels of listening comprehension, while their oral proficiency and particularly their accuracy lag behind (see Moses 2010 and Oulton 2010 for research specific to the Yup'ik region). Output and resultant opportunities for focus on form were seen as crucial elements to be covered in this course, and CALL (more specifically CMC) was identified as a mechanism to add this aspect to the teachers' repertoire. The specifics of teaching CALL are covered in the next section.

Course Goals and Content

In the class discussed here, technology is seen from a constructivist point of view as a tool that, in the hands of a skilled language teacher, offers opportunity for increased meaning-focused and form-focused engagement with the target language. Within SCT (Vygotsky 1962, 1978, 1987; Wertsch 1985), technology is viewed as one of many tools humans use within goal-directed activity. In and of themselves, these tools are neither positive nor negative. Consequently, technology use can either accelerate language shift or facilitate maintenance depending on who uses technology in what ways and for which purposes. In other words, using an iPod exclusively to listen to English-language podcasts (music, news, etc.) or using a blog to read and write posts in English fosters increased uses of English and thereby language shift toward English. However, the same technologies can also be used as tools to mediate and extend Yup'ik linguistic and cultural activity, and in turn, the activities and tools are changed through these uses. For example, creating Yup'ik-medium podcasts and writing blog posts, Facebook updates, and tweets in Yugtun creates meaningful opportunities to extend domains in which Yugtun is used, thereby fostering language maintenance. The ways these Web 2.0 applications are used may thus change the technology in very real ways. Not only will the "web space" be defined through the language used by its users, but if enough users show a demand for it, the providers might offer their interface in Yugtun. Notwithstanding larger ideological underpinning of mass media and its introduction in Indigenous contexts, it is increasingly not technology itself but users of technology who define the positioning of technology and its uses. The purpose of the class was to develop ways technology could become an agent for linguistic and cultural maintenance rather than accelerating language shift.

Despite the instructors' conviction that CALL is a potentially powerful tool for the Yup'ik teachers in our class, we were faced with a lack of published research in this area that pertains to Indigenous language learning in elementary contexts. Most research in the area of CALL is conducted in world languages (e.g., Spanish, German, Japanese, and Chinese) at the university level. Few resources currently exist that address CALL issues in elementary school settings or Indigenous language learning. The literature on uses of technology and Indigenous and endangered languages is largely limited to applications for language documentation rather than language teaching and learning. The paucity of research also posed problems for course design as the instructors searched for relevant readings that would address the needs of this student population. We decided to rely on the existing research and foundational reading from the mainstream CALL literature (for example, Erben & Sarieva 2008; Meskill 2005; Thorne 2006), with one notable exception. In her article "Words as Big as the Screen: Native American Languages and the Internet," Tracey McHenry (2002), discusses representation and participation of Indigenous languages in general and on the Internet in particular. As a positive example, she describes a website created by fourth-grade students at Tulalip Elementary School. As we discuss more fully in the analysis section, this article had a marked impact on the class.

The course was designed to provide the teachers with an overview and basic proficiency with a large range of applications to develop the ability to learn new applications as they become available. Critical thinking about how to use technology in their teaching was more important to us than technology expertise. Consequently only 35 percent of the course grade was based on the teachers' ability to produce technology examples; other assignments, such as the application paper and the thematic unit, focused more on direct classroom application and critical reflection.

The level of prior technology experience is an important factor in developing any type of technology course. Consequently we asked the teachers to complete a technology skills questionnaire and to return it three weeks before the beginning of the summer session. Many questionnaires were returned quite late, some after the first day of class. This made it difficult to tailor the course up front to match the teachers' experience and led to significant problems (as we discuss in more detail in the analysis section). A summary of demographic information and results from the technology skills questionnaire is provided in Table 3.1. The majority of the teachers (nine out of eleven) reported quite low levels of experience (mean and median of seven out of thirty on the technology self-rating scale). At the same time, two teachers (who happened to be the youngest and the only non-Indigenous students) had very high levels of experience (twenty-five and twenty-six out of a possible thirty). Based on the information obtained through the technology survey, the initial list of technologies to be introduced in this course was altered as summarized in Table 3.2.

Teaching Methodology

In designing this course, the instructors drew primarily on a constructivist, student-centered approach to learning. We wanted to draw on prior knowledge and create opportunities to engage in hands-on discovery learning experiences. Our goal was to help teachers develop critical awareness of how they might employ technologies to fit their own contexts, goals, and skills. Although we did not expect that each teacher would become an expert inthe applications we introduced, we decided that each should be exposed to and develop basic skills in a wide range of technologies. We had expected that most would enter the course with good facilities in word processing and the creation of electronic presentations (this was not true for a third of them) and had hoped to build on these skills in largely self-directed explorations with their peers and supported by the instructors. In previous courses, collaborative learning environments that engaged our learners in problem-solving tasks through dialoguing, often in Yugtun, had proven to be particularly well suited to this student population. For this reason, we planned to spend a minimum of time in teacher-fronted demonstrations. Instead, we wanted to allow the teachers to work together to figure out how to use the various technologies. This approach is supported by SCT, which posits that mediation not only by a teacher but also by peers creates meaningful opportunities for development (Donato 1994; Siekmann 2004; Vygotsky 1978; Wertsch 1985).

Based on these observations and our theoretical orientation, we applied a model of discovery and collaborative learning. The instructor modeled the initial steps for using a certain type of technology and then encouraged the teachers to explore on their own, drawing on the shared expertise within the group to discover how the programs worked and how they might be applied to language learning. An additional consideration in selecting appropriate teaching methods was that the teachers used different operating systems, browsers, and program versions. Consequently, we avoided extended whole-group formal training sessions. On a practical

Table 3.1. Demographic Information and Prior Technology Experience

Student	*Age (years)*	*Primary Language*	*Ethnicity*	*Target Language*	*Computer Platform*	*Overall Technology Skills*	*Word*	*Photo Editing*	*PowerPoint*	*Video*	*Audio*	*Blogs*	*Web Pages*	*Wiki*	*Hot Spot*	*Total (30)*
1	29	E	C	E	Mac	3	3	3	3	3	3	3	2	3	0	26
2	28	E	C	E	Mac	3	3	3	3	3	3	3	3	1	0	25
3	43	Y	Y	Y	Mac	2	2	2	2	1	1	0	0	0	0	10
4	43	Y	Y	Y	Mac	1	2	2	2	2	0	0	0	0	0	9
5	50	Y	Y	Y	PC	0	3	2	2	2	0	0	0	0	0	9
6	35	Y	Y	E	Mac	0	3	2	2	0	1	0	0	0	0	8
7	37	E	Y	E	PC	1	3	1	1	0	0	1	0	0	0	7
8	40	E	Y	E	Mac	1	1	2	0	1	0	1	0	0	0	6
9	56	Y	Y	Y	Mac	1	2	0	1	0	1	0	0	0	0	5
10	40	Y	Y	Y	Mac	1	2	1	1	0	0	0	0	0	0	5
11	59	Y	Y	Y	Mac	1	1	1	0	1	0	0	0	0	0	4
						14	25	19	17	13	9	8	5	4	0	102

Table 3.2. Applications Planned Versus Covered During the Course

Planned	*Covered*
PowerPoint	PowerPoint
Blogs: students posted daily reflective blogs about class readings	Blogs: students posted daily reflective blogs about class readings
Wiki (CALPER wiki system) one note taker posted wiki notes of daily course discussions	Wiki (CALPER wiki system) one note taker posted wiki notes of daily course discussions
Skype	Skype
WebQuests	WebQuests
Video editing (iMovie/moviemaker)	Video editing (iMovie/moviemaker)
Web page design: Dreamweaver	Web page design: Google Sites
Audio recording and publishing podcast	Audio recording and publishing podcast
Games and teacher-created individual practice (Hot Potatoes)	—
Comic strip	—

level, with everyone using different versions of a particular application or different programs altogether, it becomes impossible to lead a structured workshop. Also, the goal of the instructors was to familiarize the teachers with the basics of using the programs and then shift the focus to the potential for language learning. Developing in-depth familiarity with every feature of a particular application (for example, Microsoft Word, Microsoft PowerPoint, Apple GarageBand) can take days, weeks, and even months. Yet meaningful teaching and learning opportunities can be facilitated with only a rudimentary skill set, an idea, and the willingness to explore more advanced features later. For example, to create a simple podcast using GarageBand, one does not need to be able to work with multiple tracks and perform advance editing tasks. Furthermore, an expert technological skill set does not guarantee the creation of good language learning tasks. Consequently we had hoped to give the teachers the foundation and the confidence to further explore applications they found potentially useful with a particular emphasis on considerations for meaningful and meaning-focused language teaching and learning. What actually happened is explored in the remainder of the chapter.

Themes from Implementation and Reflection

To understand how the teachers viewed the role of technology in language teaching, we embarked on a teacher action research study (Baumann &

Duffy 2001; Mills 2003). Not only did the question originate in our own teaching practice, the research was designed to provide deeper insights into our classroom and offer opportunities for change and transformation. To this effect we collected the following data sources: teacher technology questionnaire, anonymous course evaluation forms, synthesis papers, teacher projects and final public presentations, and the instructors' field notes and debriefing session. Using the constant comparative method (Strauss & Corbin 1990), we reviewed the data sources and identified initial codes, which were refined over time. Through this process, several interconnected themes emerged from the data. In our discussion, we focus on two of these themes, each comprising two subthemes (see Table 3.3).

Theme 1: Initial Resistance to Using Technology

The data reveal that prior to this course, for some of the teachers the computer primarily functioned as a mechanism by which they and their students are monitored and controlled. As one teacher puts it: "The school district has 'gone electronic,' requiring everything from lesson planning, assessments, leave slips and attendance" (synthesis paper). This statement associates the computer with the school authority and involves things such as assessment and attendance, tasks that did not represent the positive aspects of teaching for these teachers. In other words, rather than being a teaching tool, technology has been constructed as an administrative tool forced on the teachers, creating additional work and imposing additional restrictions on them. In this situation, technology is not seen as a tool to help meet teaching needs, but as a way to meet the supervision needs of the district office.

Furthermore, technology is historically seen as an agent of language shift toward English (Krauss 1980; Moses 2010). In many villages, the arrival of the first TV set is implicated in bringing both more English and with it more mainstream (whitestream) American cultural influences. Subsequently, computers, the Internet, and electronic gaming devices

Table 3.3. Themes and Subthemes That Emerged from the Data

Theme 1: Initial Resistance to Using Technology	Theme 2: Making Technology Yup'ik
A: Technology as top-down, administrative tool	A: Creating language materials and parental involvement
B: Negotiating differences in prior technology literacy	B: Increasing opportunities for language output

(such as Xbox, Wii, Nintendo DS) continue this role: interfaces are designed in English and applications and games use English. This is extended to school materials as well, which are mass-produced for the English-speaking market, as indicated by the following excerpt: "The school has purchased several online activities for students to work on as enrichment activities for the students that supposedly match the curriculum. I have not looked into them because they are all in English; I teach in the immersion program" (synthesis paper).

Thus, the lack of prior technology skills, coupled with a sense that technology is an agent of linguistic and cultural change and a tool of "outside" control, resulted in initial resistance by some teachers to implement technology in their teaching. This view was also expressed in the course evaluation forms. In reply to the prompt: "What aspects of this class detracted from your learning?" one teacher responded: "The application/use of the technology was *frightening* and caused me to be slow to apply/practice/try it." However, the same teacher also indicated that the fact that she had a lot to learn about technology was an aspect that contributed most to her learning. "The fact that I am 'behind' in technology advances which is hindering my students—thus my need will be to not 'give up' with learning and applying the technology."

The pattern of being frustrated with the technology and also excited about its possibilities is borne out in several other course evaluations as well. The following quote is an example of this initial concern turned into excitement: "At first, I was frustrated in trying to figure out the technology part. I had a huge headache from it, but it was a learning experience" (course evaluation).

Although some teachers expressed displeasure about being asked to "figure things out for themselves," at least one saw this as an aspect of the course that contributed most to her learning. "Playing around with the programs. It was more like self discovery, student centered learning! It also gave me ideas how I can implement technology in the classroom" (course evaluation). This individual also wrote that the class was intellectually stimulating and stretched her thinking. "It was interesting to find out that technology can be implemented in second language learning. Something I've never thought about. I've learned tech stuff that I thought I would never do" (course evaluation). Here she also expressed another theme, echoed by other teachers in course evaluations and synthesis papers, that many of these students had not considered how technology might be implemented in their classrooms. The level of prior technology literacy emerged as an import factor for teacher satisfaction and will be explored in a bit more detail.

Negotiating Differences in Technology Literacy

Although the majority of the teachers only had limited prior skills in a small number of targeted technologies, the technology survey revealed that two had extensive experience. To address this disparity, we reduced the number of technologies covered (see Table 3.1) and the number of technology demonstrations. To maximize learner choice, we allowed more flexibility for the thematic unit lesson plans so that teachers no longer had to use specific applications in their lesson plans. The original syllabus required lesson plans with specific applications; one each for PowerPoint/Word/images, audio, games/drills, blog and/or wiki, and iMovie. This requirement was altered so that teachers could choose which technologies to integrate into their lesson plans, depending on their language teaching and learning needs.

These changes seemed helpful for some teachers, but for several others the modifications did not go far enough. As one teacher commented on her course evaluation form: "Technology! Lack of personal knowledge about technology and then expected to learn and produce them all in a presentation . . . not too much time to process work" (aspects that detracted from learning) and "It is not fair to be expected to learn and produce a web page with NO knowledge of technology" (suggestions to improve the course). Clearly this teacher still felt overwhelmed by the amount of technology to be learned and expresses anxiety over having to create, for example, a web page given her limited level of technology literacy at the onset of the course.

As mentioned, the instructors were happy with any level of proficiency that indicated a new set of skills. However, it is apparent from comments such as the foregoing that we had not communicated this clearly enough to the teachers. Had we been more explicit about the goals of the class, the teachers may have been more willing to play around with the technology.

On the other end of the spectrum, a few people indicated that they had not learned anything new about technology in this course because they were already familiar with this aspect of the class. Because the course requirements were changed to accommodate the teachers with less background knowledge, teachers who came to class with prior knowledge did not feel challenged.

One final excerpt from the course evaluations indicates a moderate view: "I don't know . . . maybe the frustration I felt when trying to make something work for me on my computer. But help was/is out there. And Sabine was knowledgeable and willing (more than) to help."

In short, negotiating differences in prior technology literacy was a difficult task with this particular group, and the class was only partially successful in this regard. We had hoped that teachers with stronger technology skills would help others who were just beginning to learn. However, this was only partially possible, as these teachers had their own projects to complete and often explored additional features in programs they already knew. Ultimately projects were graded on an individual rather than group level, and the stronger teachers felt no need or responsibility to support the development of their peers. This is a common finding in group work settings, one that should have been addressed from the beginning. If students are expected to help one another, structures need to be put in place that not only allow for but require collaboration for mutual success.

In the end, one instructor who was well versed in technology trying to assist eleven teachers, nine of whom had only limited prior technology skills, was frustrating at times. There was simply no time to "get to" everybody who needed help. This realization leads to two specific ideas for improvement.

IMPROVEMENT 1: COLLABORATIVE GROUP PROJECTS. One illuminating observation was that the teachers who had just learned something themselves were more likely to help others by sharing their discoveries and troubleshooting together. In essence, these groups were examples of collaborative scaffolding (Donato 1994; Siekmann 2004) as each teacher in turn took on the role of the more knowledgeable other. In these situations, learners were able to work within each other's Zone of Proximal Development (ZPD), jointly developing their technology skills. For this particular group of teachers, who overwhelmingly favor collaborative learning environments, it may have been more appropriate to assign group projects rather than individual assignments. Although we were hoping the teachers would work together, the course assignments contradicted this idea by requiring individual performance. Grouping the teachers by target language and grade level and designing assessments that would make each one accountable for the success of the whole group might well have been more conducive to collaborative learning, peer mediation, and joint problem solving.

IMPROVEMENT 2: SMALL GROUP TECHNOLOGY CENTERS. The short teacher-fronted demonstration followed by individual time to explore applications did not seem to meet the needs of this population. For the majority of the teachers, it appears that most of the technology targeted during the class was outside their ZPD, giving rise to anxiety and resistance. Many seemed afraid to "break" something or do something wrong that could not be fixed. To alleviate fear and frustration, we started to implement "technology centers" toward the end of the class. In this setting, an instructor works with a smaller group of students (three to four at a time) on particular skills in a particular program. In this way, short instructional modules allow students to follow along, help one another, and ask their personal questions. We noticed that during center time we were better able to pinpoint the teachers' actual level of development and provide mediation for them to move toward their potential level of development. This kind of teaching allows the instructor to mediate a small group of students around a small set of questions coconstructed by the group. We wish we had employed this strategy more, particularly in conjunction with group projects. An additional potential benefit for this type of modeling of this process of mediation and coconstructing the ZPD is that learners might become better able to assist one another without the presence of the instructor.

Despite the frustrations felt by both the teachers and the instructors, all the teachers learned a tremendous amount about the integration of technology in language teaching and also applied that knowledge in meaningful ways to their classroom contexts. Examples of teacher projects are shared in the next section.

Theme 2: Making Technology Yup'ik

As we started to explore potential reasons for the teachers' initial resistance to technology use, one of the issues we had to tackle was the appropriateness of using technology to teach the Yup'ik language and Yup'ik culture. It became apparent that for many of the teachers technology, on some level, represented an English environment and fostered a movement toward using English and following whitestream cultural norms. All teachers were required to use technology by the school system. This mandatory use—primarily for record keeping, assessment, and other clerical tasks—further alienated some of the teachers in the class.

Consequently, we talked about what technology means to the teachers and their students and what the lack of a strong Yup'ik presence on the Internet signals. The class readings may have inadvertently supported the idea that technology use in language learning is limited to learning ESL and to learning world languages. In fact, during one class meeting, a teacher excitedly asked: "Yeah, but how do we make it [technology] Yup'ik!?" As mentioned previously, there is a dearth of research literature in the field of CALL and Indigenous languages. Consequently, course readings largely represented the areas of ESL and world language education. The notable exception is the article "Words as Big as the Screen" (McHenry 2002). Reading and discussing this article allowed us to look at the issues of representation, access, and participation. For example, using Yugtun on the Internet can provide an environment that will represent the language as relevant and current. The current educational practice of offering Yup'ik-medium instruction to young children primarily in the early elementary grades, while older students are instructed in English, seems to suggest that Yugtun is a language for the very young (elementary school–age children) and the very old (elders), but not for older children, adolescents, and young adults. However, it is precisely this population that needs to use the language in an increasing number of domains for language revitalization to be successful (Fishman 1991). Technology might be a meaningful social environment for this demographic, because it in general and the Internet in particular are important domains for children and young adults. In retrospect it might well have been more effective to read this article early on in the class to establish the relevance of CALL to the goal of language maintenance and revitalization.

Starting with the discussion of these issues as prompted by McHenry's article, many teachers slowly changed their focus from *whether* they should use technology to *how* they could do so to provide access to target language models and authentic materials, create opportunities for meaningful output and interaction between learners, and foster parent involvement. Teacher projects and lesson plans are replete with real-life applications of technology that represent best practices in CALL. By the time teachers presented their thematic units, some of the teachers' resistance had turned to excitement, as Sikorski describes:

> The results were astounding, especially when they had to present to interested parties such as other speakers of the language, and professors. There were two basic language groups of presenters. The first group used the Yup'ik language, and the second group used english.[2] I went to the Yup'ik presentations, and was impressed at how much joy they exuded, and how they shared their newfound knowledge regarding the use of technology for language teaching and learning. It was clear the audience were both amazed and engaged, because they would ask questions about how the various technologies worked, and the students were happy to show how they were able to manipulate their voice, for instance, on GarageBand. (Siekmann & Sikorski 2009)

We now use the teachers' own words as well as their class projects to discuss the two subthemes within theme 2 (making technology Yup'ik): (a) Yup'ik language materials and parent involvement and (b) output and interaction (see Table 3.2).

SUBTHEME A: YUP'IK LANGUAGE MATERIALS AND PARENT INVOLVEMENT. All teachers created materials that use technology (Power Point, GarageBand, and iMovie) to make language input more comprehensible and more accessible to students and in some instances to parents as well. The Yup'ik-language teachers in particular emphasized the ability to bring oral stories and histories to life and into the classroom through web pages, movies, and podcasts. On the whole teachers were excited about the possibilities of bringing Yup'ik culture (hunting, fishing, gathering, Eskimo dance, berry picking, recording oral stories from elders) into the classroom, be it in English- or Yup'ik-medium instruction. Those who could not have elders visit their classrooms regularly felt that this might indeed be a way to share the elders' knowledge.

Although almost every project included an element of developing electronic target language materials through a digital slide show, a movie, or a web page, space does not allow even a brief description of every project. Therefore, we describe two projects as examplars.

Carol Oulton, who had no prior experience with web authoring, created a sophisticated Yup'ik language web page (see Figure 3.1) focusing on different facets of Yup'ik culture, for example, an iMovie about berry picking. In the video, the actors converse in Yugtun as they pick berries. This creates a powerful example of Yup'ik-medium materials for access by others. Not only does it provide language samples, it also integrates the natural environment into the teaching (see Figure 3.1).

Sally Samson expanded the idea of access in an important way by adding the potential to strengthen the home–school connection and foster parental involvement in her Yup'ik immersion kindergarten classroom. Her website contained links to PowerPoint presentations used in class to teach key vocabulary words (i.e., kinship terms). Students then record their own voices reading the words. Because this presentation is available online, it serves the additional function of informing parents of the vocabulary words learned in school. Yugtun-speaking parents can help their children learn the words. At the same time, parents who are not Yugtun speakers can learn with and from their children. Both of these uses encourage parental involvement and Yup'ik language use in the home.

The idea of using technology to perpetuate Yugtun rather than English was discussed in several synthesis papers. One teacher wrote, "I realized

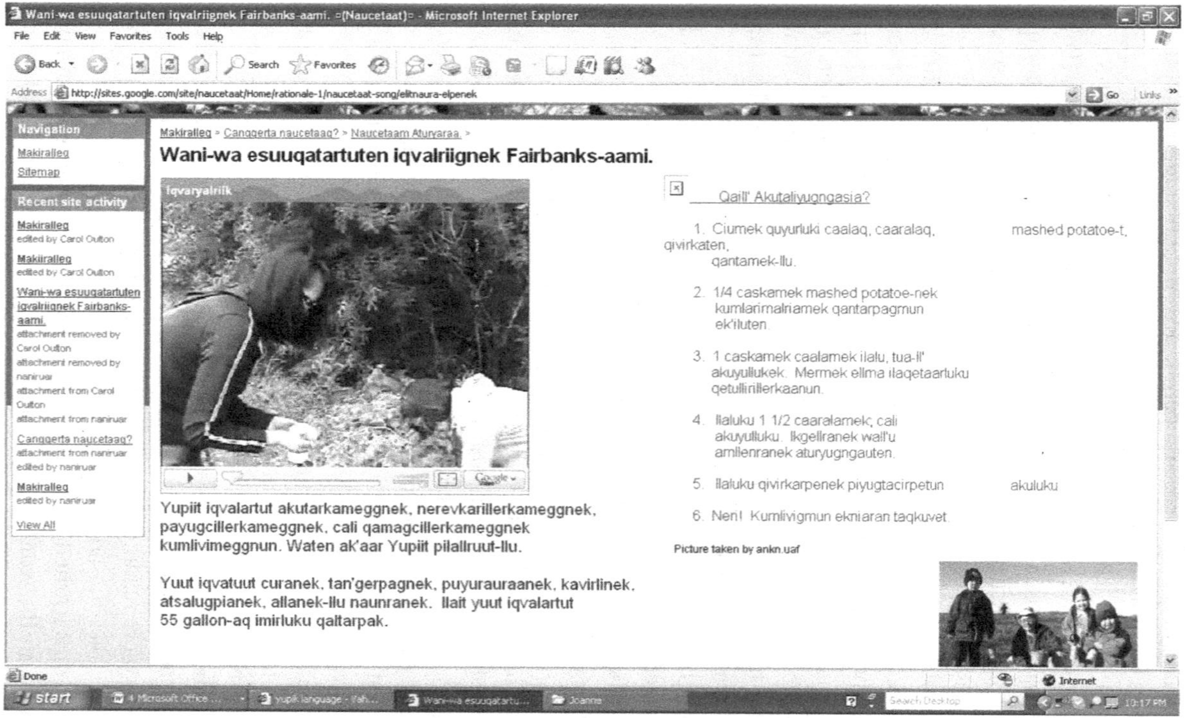

Figure 3.1. Web page example created by Carol Oulton (http://sites.google.com/site/naucetaat/Home/rationale-1/naucetaat-song/elitnaura-elpenek)

how easy it will be to record and make pages that contain actual Yup'ik conversations, words and others!" (synthesis paper). The statement shows excitement not about technology itself but about creating opportunities to use Yugtun in multiple modalities including sound, images, and video in addition to text. Teachers became aware of, and excited about, creating language materials for others to use, thereby adding to the availability of Yup'ik-language web pages. The following quote also indicates how teachers started to see technology as a teaching tool: "I didn't realize the many uses of iPod and MP3s! In iPod use, the article mentions the ability of recording conversations and slides in another language! All I knew about iPod was that it was for music listening!" (synthesis paper).

As indicated by the exclamation marks punctuating her sentences, this teacher was clearly impressed with her newfound realization that an iPod and MP3 files did not have to be in English and that they did not have to be limited to music. On the contrary, they could be used to create podcasts in any language—even Yugtun. This exemplifies the stance taken by SCT that although the tool influences the activity, the activity also influences the tool. Because the teachers had only experienced iPods used to play (English) music, they had not recognized the potential for claiming the technology for their own language. However, with this class, teachers discovered that they and their students can create podcasts and post them on the web. For example, Oulton created a Yup'ik podcast modeling a call-and-response pattern. To create two voices, one to ask the question and another to answer it, she used GarageBand to distort her own voice. When she presented her project to the campus community, the audience asked questions about how to alter voices in GarageBand, and she showed them step-by-step how to do it. Oulton had claimed the technology to such an extent that she was viewed as an expert and was able to teach her skills to others. More important, however, is the fact that during her demonstration she spoke in Yugtun, rather than English. Not only did she speak Yugtun on the recording, she also explained to the audience in Yugtun how to work the application forcefully claiming the technology for Yup'ik. Sikorski observes: "Students were asked questions in Yup'ik and answered in Yup'ik. This shows that just because technology was used and was the focus of discussion, english did not have to be used" (Siekmann & Sikorski 2009).

Oulton's and Samson's projects are wonderful examples of how to make language available online. These online resources, then, can provide authentic language input for others in the region and engage children, young adults and parents in and through Yugtun.

Moreover, Web 2.0 applications such as podcasts can do more than provide target language input for students. When the students themselves get involved in creating their own podcasts and other online content (like the students in McHenry [2002] and those in Samson's classroom), the opportunities for language output can lead to additional language learning opportunities, as discussed in the following section.

SUBTHEME B: OUTPUT AND INTERACTION. One of the issues repeatedly raised in language education (in immersion education in particular) is how to develop oral proficiency in the target language. In the context of an endangered language, such as Yugtun, this is even more pressing, because a language must be revitalized through spoken interaction. A language without speakers is, in fact, the definition of an extinct language. Consequently, teachers explored ways technology could enhance not only target language input but output as well.

The ability of CMC applications, particularly synchronous VOIP applications such as Skype, to enable learners to talk to one another in Yugtun was particularly exciting to many of the teachers, as exemplified in the following quote: "I have noticed that if the students see and hear their peers trying to speak the target language, they in turn try because they don't want to be left out! When I witnessed something like this during class this summer, I thought—how cool is this? When my instructor was talking to her child via computer, I can imagine how this would be when my students are talking to another student from another village or city" (synthesis paper).

The fact that students can talk with other students from other villages is particularly important given (1) the isolation of the villages from the urban centers and each other, and (2) the relative isolation of the immersion students even within their schools. In some villages, Yup'ik immersion and English-medium schools exist side by side, at times in the same building. The Yup'ik-medium school, however, is the one that is more "marked"; in general, instruction in English is taken to be the norm, and instruction in Yugtun is considered unusual. Consequently, being able to connect to same-age peers in other villages who are also learners of their ancestral language offers great opportunities for community building and meaningful exchanges in Yugtun. In addition, as the following excerpt indicates, one teacher felt that this type of learning would be very motivating to learners: "I could also imagine students networking with other students via iChat with other fellow immersion students (simultaneously) who actually are speaking the language to them, and for the students to hear students their age speaking the Yup'ik language. I am hoping that when this happens the students will be motivated to actually try to use more Yup'ik" (synthesis paper).

As discussed in the following section, the teachers' comments about the potential for technology to support Yup'ik language maintenance and revitalization rather than language shift to English did not remain an idle idea stated in a paper for the benefit of the course instructors.

Lessons Learned and Next Steps

In summary, there was some resistance to the application of technology in teaching due in part to technology being constructed by the schools as a clerical rather than instructional tool. Additionally, mass media as an outside, largely English influence has been one factor in language shift. The teachers' relatively low level of prior technology skills also resulted in low levels of confidence and concerns about class performance. As we started to redefine technology, most of the teachers started to develop confidence and technology skills, and all of them created activities for their classrooms that were grounded in Yup'ik culture and values.

The teachers became familiar with the basic functionality of a variety of tools and developed basic facility in the hands-on skills needed to use them in their teaching. They demonstrated these skills in their presentations at the end of the semester. The thematic units developed also represent some of the best practices of CALL by making choices that are appropriate to the linguistic and cultural situation and needs. As a result of taking this class, teachers are being seen as local leaders not just in language teaching but in the area of using technology, resulting in at least one in-service presentation by a teacher.

Despite the fact that the class was successful in our final analysis, we feel that the goals in terms of which technology skills to develop may have been too ambitious. The goal was to expose the teachers to a wide range of technologies so they would be able to select the tools that best fit their needs, skills, and goals. However, our expectations should have been made clearer to the teachers.

In the end, the class seemed successful in redefining technology as a potential tool to teach Yugtun in linguistically and culturally appropriate ways. Teachers began to use technology to increase the use of Yugtun rather than English. This newfound insight is expressed by one teacher: "In taking this class this summer, I have realized how I can use technology to assist in language learning for the students. It never occurred to me how this would benefit and enhance language acquisition" (synthesis paper).

Another teacher reiterates the potential to harness the power of technology to reverse language shift, but she also acknowledges the amount of time and energy involved in creating sound CALL applications. "It will take a long time and energy, but thinking how technology has already made an impact in the Yup'ik society, it is important that Yup'ik language teachers like myself need to practice and learn way[s] in which we can make use of the technology to help in maintaining and revitalizing the Yup'ik language" (synthesis paper).

In conclusion, one of the most significant outcomes of this class is that teachers recognized the importance of continuing and expanding the types of collaborations that emerged around the use of technology in Yup'ik-medium schools. One of the teachers wrote: "Networking with other immersion programs sounds exciting and workable for me and my students. In fact, during one of our class discussions, my colleagues and I discussed with excitement how beneficial networking would be in our programs. We made a pact then that we will follow through with our plan" (synthesis paper).

The pact has resulted in a collaborative grant effort (Piciryaramta Elicungcallra [Teaching Our Way of Life through Our Language]; US Dept of Education grant #S356090066) to create technology-infused thematic units for the Yup'ik-medium schools in the Lower Kuskokwim and Lower Yukon School Districts that are linguistically and culturally appropriate to Yup'ik students and target the Alaska state standards in reading, writing, social studies, and science. Eight of the SLATE graduates are continuing the conversations started during this class and are taking active roles in the development of materials in their districts.

Ultimately, the transformation from seeing technology as a burden to perceiving its potential to support the teachers' goals of language teaching and language revitalization was brought about through the teachers' discovery of their own abilities and capabilities when given the tools to incorporate their knowledge, experience base, and language. Exploring and discovering together the potential of CALL to support their classroom and community goals has given all the teachers, particularly the Yup'ik immersion teachers, the tools to "make technology Yup'ik" and take leadership roles in local materials development.

Notes

1. Additionally, few publisher-created resources are available for Indigenous languages. Rosetta Stone offers its software package in six endangered languages of North America (see http://www.rosettastone.com/global/endangered); this offering in no way represents the state of the art of CALL as defined by researchers and practitioners in the field.

2. Sikorski writes *english* without the normal capitalization as a way to symbolically grant greater power to Indigenous peoples and their languages.

CHAPTER FOUR

On Becoming a "Literate" Person

Meaning Making with Multiliteracies and Multimodal Tools

Joan Parker Webster and Theresa Arevgaq John

"Reinventing" in the colonizer's tongue and turning those images around to mirror an image of the colonized to the colonizers as a process of decolonization indicates that something is happening, something is emerging and coming into focus that will politicize as well as transform literary expression.

HARJO AND BIRD (1997, P. 22)

In this chapter, we tell the story of the conception, development, and implementation of a summer intensive master's-level course titled "Multiliteracies in Second Language Classrooms." By *multiliteracies* we mean an expansion of the traditional view of school-based literacy that reaches beyond the linguistic realm of reading and writing. The overall process supporting the evolution of the course is rooted in dialogic discussions among the stakeholders (doctoral student and coinstructor/adviser, faculty member, and master's students) participating in a collaborative research group, Multiliteracies Graduate Research Collaborative (GRC), a subgroup of the Second Language Acquisition Teacher Education (SLATE) program. These discussions, which stem from ongoing conversations conducted during sessions taking place each semester, are concerned with theoretical and methodological issues related to teaching and learning multiliteracies in diverse cultural and linguistic contexts, particularly those situated in Indigenous communities. Thus, using this dialogic process, we initiate a new dialogue between the notion of multiliteracies described in Western academic literature and Indigenous multimodal methodologies of traditional oral storytelling, music, dance, and culturally based subsistence activities, which provided the basis for the summer course.

We begin with an overview of the methodology used for the data collected and analyzed in this chapter. Next, we present our conceptual framework supporting the new dialogue developed in this course and continue the discussion with descriptions of the course design and instructional procedures stemming from that framework. We discuss the themes that emerged through data collected from our course activities and discussions. We conclude with reflections on the course that provide new directions for further dialogic conversations.

Methodology

Theoretical Framework

A primary principle that guides our research is bringing together multiple cultural perspectives, theories, and methodologies to gain greater understanding of the commonalities and differences across diverse knowledge systems. This principle is important because, in our view, the inclusion of methodological and theoretical perspectives other than the traditional Western view can help ease the apprehension and mistrust felt by Indigenous communities toward university-based research. In many instances, this mistrust stems from constituted power relations that privilege the established academic community over those communities and individuals often considered *subjects* in university-based research. In such power relationships, members of disadvantaged groups are often willing to set aside their mistrust and accept the goodwill extended by the privileged, but they are also aware that such goodwill on the part of the privileged groups is not enough to overcome the assumptions and attitudes that have evolved over years of power and privilege (Narayan 1988). Therefore, we find it imperative to situate our research within a framework that supports a real dialogue between members of groups with heterogeneous composition, such as those representing the Western academy and those representing the Indigenous community. The Western theoretical framework that most closely fits this notion of dialogue is Jürgen Habermas's theory of communicative action, in particular the notion of *communicative action oriented toward understanding* (Habermas 1987), because it privileges a notion of understanding that can occur only in a negotiated way on the terms of the people involved in the communicative act. In our collaborative research experiences with Yup'ik communities, we have discovered that the notion of communicative action oriented toward understanding, based in working toward a collaborative negotiation of meaning within the group, also underscores the theory and practice of communicative interactions Yup'ik elders employ in their epistemological, theoretical, and methodological discussions that take place at community dance performances, storytelling events, and elder meetings. Therefore, Habermas's theory of communicative action seems an appropriate framework for opening a space for dialogue among different academies situated in and out of university contexts (Parker Webster & John 2010).

We also use a critical ethnographic methodology put forth by Phil Francis Carspecken (1996). The notion of "critical" when attached to research has two distinct yet interconnected meanings. *Critical* can refer to the value orientation of the researcher—often referred to as a criticalist—which is characterized by a focus on social justice issues and the betterment of oppressed and marginalized groups. A *critical methodology* refers to the epistemological principles that underpin a critical approach to research. These principles include such ideas as that all thought is mediated by power relations that are historically and socially constituted and that statements of "fact," which are endemic to all research, cannot be isolated from the domain of values. Therefore, research can never be strictly neutral or objective. A critical orientation does not determine the "facts" we uncover in our research. Rather, it guides the reasons we conduct the research and what contexts and people we involve in our research study. Critical epistemology does not imply or guarantee that the facts we may find in our research match what we as critical researchers want to find, and the value orientations of the researcher may not exactly match the value orientations suggested by the research findings. Thus, by recognizing the interrelation between critical epistemological principles that guide critical research methodology and criticalist value orientations, researchers can better understand the facts or findings of their research.

Finally, using James Paul Gee's (2007) theoretical framework, we examine the holistic notion of language that includes not only language-in-use, or discourse (lowercase *d*) but also nonlanguage aspects, or Discourse (capital *D*), which are "gestures, clothes, actions, interactions, symbols, tools, technologies, values, attitudes, beliefs and emotions" (p. 7) that allow us to enact specific identities that are associated with language-in-use.

Participants

Participants in this study (see also Chapter 1) included nine Yup'ik Eskimo and two non-Native female teachers, as well as the GRC faculty adviser (Joan Parker Webster) and Alaska Native doctoral candidate (Theresa

Arevgaq John) who coinstructed the course. Of these, eight of the Yup'ik teachers and the coinstructor/doctoral candidate are fluent Yup'ik first language speakers. Data consist of field notes, class artifacts and videotapes of class activities and presentations, instructors' planning and debriefing sessions, and teacher exit interviews. From these data, we have identified five emerging themes: (1) consonance and dissonance in multimodal genre, (2) semiotics of gesture, (3) technology as a double-edged tool, (3) cross-cultural transmediations, and (5) pedagogy from the "inside out." These are discussed in following sections. We begin by laying the foundation for the content and methodology of the course with an outline of the conceptual framework.

Conceptual Framework

The genesis of the conceptual framework for the class emerged in early planning conversations between John and Parker Webster about the content and format for the regular Multiliteracies GRC meetings. For these meetings, which commenced in fall 2007, we developed an initial reading list to provide some basic descriptions of the notion of multiliteracies and form the basis for initial discussions. After a few meetings, some of the teachers began to suggest readings they had come across in their research projects. As the meetings progressed, these readings became part of our discussions, and the teachers took on more and more responsibility for choosing relevant readings and leading the discussions. These topics and discussions coalesced around four broad areas (described in detail later): (1) sociocultural theory; (2) multiliteracies and transmediation; (3) *yuuyaraq*, *quliraq/qanemciq*, and *yuraq*; and (4) critical pedagogy. When we began thinking about the rationale, content and instructional strategies for the multiliteracies summer course (2008), these four areas provided a natural starting point for developing the content and format/procedures for the class. Thus, the conceptual framework underlying the conception, development, and implementation of the course stemmed from these interrelated and overlapping theoretical and pedagogical perspectives.

Sociocultural Theory

A primary tenet of sociocultural theory is that human thought—the process of thinking—is the basis for human learning. Specifically, we draw from Lev Vygotsky's (1978) theory of human development and learning, which emphasizes the primacy of the social nature of all human activity and situates learning within social contexts. We interpret this to mean that learning takes place in the context of collaborative activity, which involves multiple cultural resources that work together to create ranges of potentials within Zones of Proximal Development (ZPD)[1] that emerge through group interaction (Parker Webster, Wiles, Civil, & Clark 2005).

This perspective on learning through collaborative activity has also been referred to as joint productive activity (Tharp & Gallimore 1988), which reflects a socially mediated process of coparticipation and colearning (Gutierrez, Baquedano-Lopez, Alvarez, & Chiu 1999). Thus, within this perspective, collaborative activities involving teacher–student(s) and student–student discussions are socially mediated contexts for learning. Through this approach, we move away from a pedagogical model that relies solely on "directive scaffolding" to a model that includes more "supportive scaffolding" (Gallas 1995; Wilkinson & Silliman 2000) in which the student is allowed an ownership role in her own learning.[2] This notion of collaborative activity or joint productive activity that includes supportive scaffolding is an important piece in our framework because it is closely aligned to the ways teaching and learning (known as *elitnaurista-llu atuunem maligtaqulluk*) are theorized and practiced within Yup'ik communities.

Another aspect of Vygotskian theory of human development and learning is the idea that tools and signs mediate our thought processes. In such a theory, a tool can be language, and it can also be a counting system, or music, or visual art. Tools, such as language, construct signs, such as words. The cultural values of a group are represented in the sign systems they use to assist them in human activity, communication, and the formation of social structures and relationships. The extent to which individual members of cultural groups internalize the values of their group's cultural way of knowing depends on the degree of consonance members have with the cultural tools they use to mediate individual as well as collective development (Smagorinsky 1995). This notion that tools and signs are mediators of human thought processes is closely related to the theoretical perspective of multiliteracies and transmediation.

Multiliteracies and Transmediation

The concept of multiliteracies is predicated on the notion that literacy and literacy practices are always socially situated and ideologically formed

(Gee 1996; Luke 2000; New London Group 1996). As such, being citizens in today's social, cultural, and economic worlds requires us to negotiate a variety of multimodal texts that use a multiplicity of discourses—those bits of language that are used within a larger Discourse (Gee 1996, 2007). We draw from Gunther Kress's (2000) description in which multimodality can be viewed in three distinct and related ways. First, all texts are multimodal; however, one modality can dominate. For example, a children's picture book contains visual images as well as written language. Second, there are texts and objects of a semiotic nature that exist in a mode or modes other than the (multi)mode of language, such as an oil painting or orchestral music. Third, there are systems of communication and representation that are designated by culture to be multimodal. For example, in the Yup'ik culture, *qanemciq* and *quliraq* (oral stories) and *yuraq* (Yupik dance) are multimodal.

As the New London Group (2000) states, this calls for an extension of the idea and scope of literacy and literacy pedagogy to take into account the context of culturally and linguistically diverse and increasingly globalized societies. It also requires a semiotic approach, which means examining how meaning is constructed through all kinds of signs—pictures, gestures, music, mathematics—not just the linguistic sign system, which is heavily privileged in school-based education. In other words, multiliteracies are based in the idea that representation and communication occur through the use of multiple sign and symbol systems (such as Yup'ik storyknife symbols; numeric symbols; the sign system of visual art composed of line, texture, etc.; Yup'ik dance gestures) that humans use to construct meaning and interpret knowledge. In addition, given our ever-expanding notion of what a text is and what form it takes, literacy pedagogy must also address the ongoing development of multiple text forms associated with information and multimedia technologies.

As previously stated, an extended notion of literacy as expressed in multiliteracies requires a semiotic approach, which allows us to study how meaning is made through multiple sign systems, how different signs relate to each other, and how they are manipulated. Because multiliteracies incorporates multiple sign systems, transmediation—the process of how meaning is constructed and reconstructed as it moves from one sign system to another—provides us a way to frame a pedagogy that has multiliteracies at its core. When conceptualized through semiotic representation and transmediation, multiliteracies allow for meaning making across multiple sign systems. Thus, rather than ask what a child knows, we can ask how many ways are available for this child to know (Halliday 1975).

Yuuyaraq, Quliraq/Qanemciq, *and* Yuraq

The third perspective is grounded in the Yup'ik ontological and epistemological framework of *yuuyaraq*, which means the way of being a human. This "way" involves the concept of the interconnectedness of the physical environment, the people, and the spiritual world. These three realms must work together—not in isolation—for a human to be prepared to successfully live the Yup'ik way of life. Integral to *yuuyaraq* is a methodology represented in Yup'ik oral narrative. Oral narratives represented in *qanemciq* and *quliraq*[3] articulate Yup'ik epistemology through an ongoing oral account of knowledge, and they also are a methodology used to pass that knowledge on to future generations. Similarly, *yuraq* (Yup'ik dancing, singing, and drumming) has played a functional role in organizing and maintaining various societal structures (e.g., kinship, social, political, subsistence/economic, and spirituality) within the Yup'ik culture. Thus, stories and dance perform a number of important social functions within Yup'ik society. They are a way to preserve a people's historical and cultural memory and a way to connect the past and the present. They can also provide instruction not only in cultural values and norms—how to act—but also in ways of survival and tasks of everyday living.

Critical Pedagogy

The fourth perspective is critical pedagogy. By *critical pedagogy*, we refer to the interactive relationship between teaching and learning and theory and practice, called *praxis*, developed by Paolo Freire (2000). This relationship reflects a transformative process that can help us challenge and reflect on our long-held assumptions about what we view as the status quo. Thus, this active, transformative process can help us question our theories about and practices in the world and act on them. Based on a synthesis of work in the field of critical pedagogy (Darder 2008; hooks 1994; Kincheloe 2008; McLaren 2007; Seale & Slapin 2006), we used the following principles to form the basis of the instructional practices implemented in our class:

- Use local knowledge and practices.
- Provide opportunities for students to become critical producers of meanings and texts.
- Provide tools that can help students critically question systems of cultural domination and transform themselves from objects to subjects, passive to active.
- Illuminate the relationship among knowledge, authority, and power.

However, even with these important principles as a foundation, we also know the importance of being in an ongoing reflexive mode as teachers and learners. Thus, maintenance of a critical pedagogy for all stakeholders requires a continual and critical reflective stance on theory and practice in general as well as on our own individual praxis.

Methods and Modes

We created the theoretical framework for our course with the primary goal of presenting the concept of multiliteracies as inherent in all of our social and cultural practices and therefore integral to the language and literacy pedagogies of the teachers (both Yugtun and English) who would participate in the class. Even though not all of the teachers were involved in teaching the Yup'ik language directly, they all taught in rural contexts in which cultural activities (e.g., Yup'ik dancing, subsistence hunting and gathering) were still practiced and the heritage language was still spoken by community members to varying degrees. The other unifying factor was that the student populations of all the teachers' classrooms were predominantly Yup'ik/Alaska Native. Therefore, as we planned the course, we focused on incorporating Yup'ik epistemology, traditional pedagogy and cultural activities, and heritage language as a medium for instruction in tandem with Western pedagogical theories and practices to develop course content and methods.

To accomplish this, our approach for teaching the content of the class included both Yup'ik and Western theories and methodologies, such that we would present each perspective through a collaborative dialogue. For example, when examining literary genre, Parker Webster would present the Western literary categories (fiction, nonfiction, traditional, etc.) and their characteristics, and in a dialogic format John would present the Yup'ik storytelling "genre" represented by *qanemciq* and *quliraq* in both Yugtun and English. Then, together we facilitated group discussions about various aspects and similarities and differences across both Yup'ik and Western notions of genre. Procedurally, we also facilitated group work to allow for the Yup'ik speakers to conduct their discussions, create artifacts, and make class presentations in Yugtun. Thus, our rationale and intent to blend Yup'ik and Western knowledge systems and pedagogical approaches seemed to suggest the following methods and modes for implementing the course content: story circles and storyknifing/*yaaruiq*, Yup'ik dance/*yuraq*, and reader's theater, theater of the oppressed, and tableaux.

*Story Circles and Storyknifing/*Yaaruiq

Supportive scaffolding and collaborative learning, key components in our articulated sociocultural perspective, were the basis for one of our collaborative discussion methods called story circles. Briefly stated, story circles are student-facilitated discussion groups, composed of four or five students, in which individual students or partners take on roles and responsibilities for various aspects of the topic under discussion. Story circles are similar to literature circles (Daniels 1994, 2001) in many ways. However, the story circles model developed here is grounded in the Yup'ik cultural activity of storyknifing, which has been an integral part of Yup'ik narrative tradition for centuries. Storyknifing (*yaaruiq*) is an activity in which little girls tell each other stories based on the traditional stories told to them by their older sisters, mothers, and expert storytellers. As a girl tells her story, she draws symbols that visually represent the events in a small patch of mud or sand using a storyknife—a tool specifically made for this activity.

In the story circles method, we incorporated the procedure of oral discussion accompanied by visual representation through writing, graphic organizers, drawings, symbols, and so on carried out in a small-group format so that all students can contribute to the discussion and visual representation at the same time. The primary difference between story circles and literature circles is the emphasis on collaborative group work in carrying out the duties associated with the various story circle roles. In the story circle method, small groups initially collaborate on carrying out the duties of each role, rather than relying on individual students acting as the sole facilitator of the role. Story circles also use tools that can accommodate multiple drawings or other graphics, such as chart paper, on which all students can brainstorm and record their initial ideas and responses.

Story Circles also employs the learning strategies that are part of learning and retelling stories through *yaaruiq*. The following narrative by Evelyn Yanez describes these strategies:

> We would listen to Annie Blue tell her stories and then the next day, we would sit and storyknife what we remembered about the story. Whoever remembered most of the story and was ready to tell the story would be the storyteller, and we all sat and storyknifed the story. That's how we learned the story, by retelling the story over and over again and storyknifing. Sometimes my mom would tell the story to me and I would be the storyteller and tell it to other kids while we all storyknifed. It was through storyknifing that we would tell what we

> learned. Sometimes we didn't know certain words, and we would ask for help. For example, if I didn't know the word for arrow, my cousin would draw the symbol for arrow and then I would learn the word. This is how we learned new vocabulary. We also asked each other questions. For example, I might ask my cousin where she thought Iluvaktuq was hunting when he got the giant caribou, and she might draw and describe a place on the river. It was this way that we could respond to the story and add details that came from our own images about the setting. These details connected to our own personal experiences and this helped us learn to retell the story. Sometimes our questions about the story would lead to other discussions outside the story. For example, I might ask about what kind of fish Iluvaktuq ate, and we would talk about all the different kinds of fish that lived in the Togiak region and where you would find them. And, while we were having these discussions we were also storyknifing. (Parker Webster, Yanez, & Andrew-Ihrke 2007, pp. 12–13)

In summary, then, the story circles method and mode that we used for collaborative discussions about the course readings, which included both research-based journal articles and other topic-focused texts, as well as children's literature, Yup'ik elder narratives, films, oral storytelling tapes, and other culturally based "texts," draws from the procedures and strategies used in traditional storyknifing practices with a role structure that defines specific duties carried out by group members (see Table 4.1).

Yuraq/*Yup'ik Dance*

The notions of movement, gesture, and interpretation of meaning through kinesthetic performance are key elements in a multiliteracies approach. These are also key elements in *yuraq* or Yup'ik dance. The traditional Yup'ik dance instruction used in the class included learning the basic gestures and movements associated with various dances, the structure of the song composition, and how to represent different choreographic symbols. The goal was for students to understand the organization and structures of *yuraq* and how drumming, music, and gesture/movements are developed using the terminologies associated with Yup'ik dance. In the class, John outlined a theoretical and sociohistorical framework for the diverse cyclic dance styles, *agayuliyararput*, *kevgigyaraq*, and *ciuqitet*, to provide a context for the dance instruction of various dances. *Agayuliyararput* is a masking ceremony that is no longer practiced. It is defined as a form of prayer because it was a method to ask the animal spirits to grant food items. *Kev-*

Table 4.1. Storyknifing Strategies and Story Circle Roles/Duties

Storyknifing Strategies	*Story Circle Roles/Duties*
Retell and summarize the story by using elements, such as characters, setting, plot, and moral	Summarizer: facilitates summarizing what the story or text is about
Ask about new words to learn new vocabulary	Word gatherer: facilitates vocabulary/word study
Ask questions of others in the storyknifing event about the story	Questioner: facilitates asking questions about the story or text
Talk about details that connected personal experiences to the story	Connector: facilitates making personal connections to the story or text
Draw visual images or symbols representing events in the story	Interpreter: facilitates interpreting the story or text in a nonlinguistic medium or multimodal form (drawing, dance, tableaux, etc.)
Storyknifer chooses which traditional story she will retell	Reader: facilitates choosing a favorite passage from the story or text to read aloud; can be combined with interpreter role/duties

giryaraq was also called a messenger feast, in which communities exchanged gifts. These involved exchanges either between women and men in the village or between villages. *Ciuqitet* are the modern dance styles. The *ciuqitet* are the only dances that have been maintained.

We also explored the choreographic symbols and discussed the functional roles of gestures as signs and symbols that are directly related to the music composition. The students were instructed in new dances every day to build their repertoire of traditional Yup'ik dances and also build their knowledge of common symbols, gestures, and choreographic structure so that they could develop an understanding of the syntax and vocabulary of the structure and symbolic signs/gestures in the dances. It was also a goal that through learning these symbols, gestures, and choreographic structures they could use these as tools to teach students how to create a song and dance as well as transmediate their learning and understanding of an oral story, nonfiction essay, concept, and so on into another mode of interpretation.

Theater of the Oppressed, Reader's Theater, and Tableaux

As a dialogic partner to the performativity and multimodality of Yup'ik dance/*yuraq*, we drew from three dramatic processes: reader's theater, tableaux, and theater of the oppressed. Although all have been used in Western-based systems (e.g., education and performing arts), Augusto Boal (1979) developed theater of the oppressed (TO) primarily as a medium for social and political change. TO has its roots in Freire's critical pedagogy. Freire used the term *banking education* to describe a pedagogical model in which the teacher bestows or "deposits" the gift of knowledge to passive learners, who are considered blank slates and come to education without any prior knowledge. Like Freire, who challenged this one-way transmission model in education, Boal challenged the monologic model in the theatre. Boal coined the term *spect-actor* to describe the active role in which members of the audience engage as they consciously cross the boundary between watching as a spectator and taking part in the action as an actor.

Our goal was to use TO as a critical framework for the teachers in the class to challenge issues related to authenticity, accuracy, cultural appropriateness, bias, or hegemony in children's books representing the Indigenous/Native experience. To implement TO, we used the dramatic tools of reader's theater and tableaux. In reader's theater, a portion of a text is read aloud as a script. Individual and chorus parts are designated and assigned. The reading is performed, usually without props or movement. In tableaux, a short passage of a text, one portraying a physical action or emotion, is read aloud, usually by one person or narrator. Actors represent the actions and/or emotions of the characters in the passage, and in ensemble they create a freeze-framed, visual representation of the passage as it is read aloud. TO was implemented by audience members stopping the performance to pose critical questions about the passage or scene to the readers or actors. Another strategy was for audience members to suggest alternatives or changes to the narrative or scene by tapping a reader or actor on the shoulder and inserting their own thoughts or actions into the passage or scene. Both strategies were designed to initiate critical discussions about issues related to choosing and using children's books and other teaching materials in the classroom.

Emerging Themes

After an initial analysis of the data collected in the course, we identified emerging categories that represent five broad themes: (1) consonance and dissonance in multimodal genre, (2) semiotics of gesture, (3) technology as a double-edged tool, (4) cross-cultural transmediations, and (5) pedagogy from the "inside out." In this section, we provide a general overview of the themes presented in Table 4.2. Then we describe how our analysis revealed nuances of practice that illustrated distinct differences within each of the themes. We then give an overview of the first three themes (consonance and dissonance in multimodal genre, semiotics of gesture, and technology as a double-edged tool) and how they were enacted in the class. Finally, we take a closer look at the two remaining themes (cross-cultural transmediations and pedagogy from the inside out), using examples from teachers' in-class discussions, presentations, and drafts of written assignments.

Table 4.2 presents each theme, along with its primary characteristics. We further analyzed the data within each theme for evidence of connections to our conceptual framework; the connections are listed in the Conceptual Framework column. Direct links to the conceptual framework emerged in class discussions, students' presentations, and written drafts of class assignments. For example, in one class activity where students compiled and presented a checklist of things to look for when choosing children's books representing Native children, one student remarked, "This activity is critical pedagogy in action." More tacit links were demonstrated through class activities and discussions of practical applications and defining elements of the concept. Links were also manifested in instructor debriefing sessions, which occurred after each class session, in which John and Parker Webster reflected on class activities and discussions to see if the conceptual framework was actually being implemented. The order of the concepts listed in Table 4.2 is based on data analysis that takes into account both the frequency of actual reference to the concept (terminology) and instances of the concepts' practical applications evidenced in classroom discussions, activities, and written assignments. Because of the interrelatedness of the conceptual framework, the order is perhaps better viewed as a horizon of foregrounded and backgrounded concepts rather than hierarchical. As illustrated in Table 4.2, the link to sociocultural theory is presented in brackets because it appeared as the most backgrounded in all of the themes. In our view, this is most likely caused by the limited references in class readings dealing directly with this topic. Though the notion of sociocultural theory was embedded in the readings on multiliteracies, the concept of multiliteracies was more foregrounded and more directly referred to in teacher discussions than the concept of sociocultural theory. As you will see in an example later (see Oulton's Rationale), the closest link to sociocultural theory is a reference to "sociocultural practice," which is used in the context of the teacher's description of a

Table 4.2. Themes and Identifying Characteristics

Emerging Theme	*Defining Characteristics*	*Connection to Conceptual Framework*
Consonance and dissonance in multimodal genre	1. Noting of similarities and differences in Western/Yup'ik notions of genre 2. Critical reviewing of representations of Indigenous experiences in western literature by non-Indigenous authors 3. Challenging inclusion and exclusion of "texts" in educational settings (e.g., using *quliraq*, *qanemciq*, and *yuraq* in curriculum) 4. Creating new "texts" by including or combining elements of Western and Yup'ik genre	Multiliteracies, critical pedagogy, *yuuyaraq*, *quliraq/qanemciq*, and *yuraq* [sociocultural theory]
Semiotics of gesture	1. Noting semantic, syntactic, and pragmatic features in gestures signifying meaning in *yuraq*, tableau, visual art/illustrations 2. Collecting a lexicon of symbols/gestures for creating new dances 3. Recognizing commonalities between gestures from one sign system/mode to another (e.g., *yuraq*, tableaux) and gestural symbols and visual graphic symbols (e.g., storyknife symbols)	Multiliteracies, *yuuyaraq*, *quliraq/qanemciq*, and *yuraq* [sociocultural theory]
Technology as a double-edged tool	1. Challenges of learning and using technology as a tool 2. Recognizing specific technologies software, hardware, etc. as tools for heritage language teaching and maintenance 3. Finding the appropriate fit between tool/mode and language/culture	Multiliteracies, *yuuyaraq*, *quliraq/qanemciq*, and *yuraq* [sociocultural theory]
Cross-cultural transmediations	1. Discovery of multimodalities that transcend cultural boundaries 2. Incorporating multiliteracies and multimodalities across culturally based and school-based disciplines 3. Transmediating using a variety of sign systems/modalities rooted in diverse cultural contexts	*Yuuyaraq*, *quliraq/qanemciq* and *yuraq*, multiliteracies [sociocultural theory]
Pedagogy from the inside out	1. Critically examining epistemological/methodological connection between pedagogical theory and practice 2. Challenging status quo of school-based pedagogy 3. Developing methodologies from *yuuyaraq* (epistemology) 4. Starting with *yuuyaraq* (inside) to create a "third space" for Indigenous/school-based pedagogy 5. Developing curriculum and materials based in multiliteracies	*Yuuyaraq*, *quliraq/qanemciq*, and *yuraq*, critical pedagogy, multiliteracies [sociocultural theory]

cultural practice as an example of multiliteracies. This notion of multiliteracies as situated in sociocultural theory and practice was embedded in class readings.

We included these links to the conceptual framework in our data analysis in an effort to examine if and how the theories on which the course was based actually played out in practice. This was important to our overall evaluation of the planning and implementation of the class to understand what worked, the challenges and the changes we would make to the syllabus, and the course implementation. We also wanted to examine the efficacy of our theories about learning and pedagogy in terms of our own learning and instructional practices as well as the learning and teaching practices of the teachers in the class. As illustrated in Table 4.2, the elements of the conceptual framework emerged in the discussions, responses, and practices reflected in the data. In the next section we discuss how the themes, while forming an interrelated whole, also have distinct nuances of practice that give them unique qualities.

Nuances of Practice

The identifying characteristics of the themes presented in Table 4.2 are interrelated parts of a whole. The themes are also conceptually interrelated, as illustrated in the Conceptual Framework column. At the same time, each theme contains unique nuances that are reflected in the actual practices, which are listed under the theme's Defining Characteristics. These nuances contributed to the identification of five distinct themes. For example, in the consonance and dissonance theme, a distinguishing nuance of practice was the critical focus. Students developed their own critical perspectives from articles and reviews by Indigenous scholars as well as from their own cultural knowledge and experiences with *quliraq* and *qanemciq*. When reviewing picture storybooks that were adapted from Alaska Native and American Indian (AN/AI) stories by Native and non-Native authors, students actively engaged in determining authenticity, accuracy, and issues of bias present in the texts. Thus, in practice, developing their own critical perspectives helped them critically evaluate and choose AN/AI picture books for use in their classrooms. This perspective also helped them address the issues of authenticity and accuracy as they created picture storybooks and other multimodal texts using Yup'ik oral stories and Yup'ik dance. (For more discussion of the process of transmediation, see the following discussion of the transmediation theme.) In addition, developing a critical perspective also provided teachers with a voice to challenge the Western print-based literacy curriculum often privileged in schools. Thus, although both the defining characteristics of practice in the transmediation and consonance and dissonance themes involve transmediation, or movement from one sign system and/or modality to another to communicate meaning, the distinguishing nuance of the consonance and dissonance theme is the critical stance employed by students; the distinguishing nuance of practice in the transmediation theme is primarily based in the process of transmediating from one sign system to another.

Similarly, while the themes semiotics of gesture and cross-cultural transmediation share their foundation in the theory of semiotics, the distinguishing nuance of practice for semiotics of gesture is the greater theoretical focus on structural analysis. For example, as stated earlier, teachers discovered semantic, syntactic, and pragmatic features of gestures in Yup'ik dance (*yuraq*). In other words, like words in the linguistic sign system, gestures are signifiers representing animals, people, places, objects, and so on, and these words can be arranged in a syntactic order that both constructs and construes meaning situated within a cultural context. The concept of transmediation took on a more analytical focus in this theme as teachers learned to identify and compare similarities and differences between the form and functional attributes of gestures in one sign system/mode and another (e.g., *yuraq* and tableaux) and also between gestural symbols of *yuraq* and visual/graphic symbols found in storyknife lexicons. In contrast, in the cross-cultural transmediation theme, actively engaging in the transmediating process was the nuance of practice. In other words, in the semiotics of gesture theme, theoretical analysis was foregrounded, and in the cross-cultural transmediation theme, the practical application was foregrounded.

Finally, in the theme of technology as a double-edged tool, the focus is on technology as a multiliteracies tool. Although related in theory to the other themes by the overarching concept of multiliteracies, this theme contains elements not outwardly manifested in the others. These are characterized by overt behaviors exhibiting tension, anxiety, and resistance that were exhibited by all the teachers. In the following section we summarize the defining characteristics of the first three themes in terms of how these were enacted in class discussions and activities.

Consonance and Dissonance in Multimodal Genre

In the theme of consonance and dissonance in multimodal genre, participants used a critical approach to examine and analyze the Western constructs of literary elements, genre, and the notion of *text* in juxtaposition with Indigenous/Yup'ik literary traditions. Many of the teachers, both Yup'ik and non-Yup'ik, discovered that the *culturally appropriate* literary texts used in their classrooms were predominantly adaptations in English of traditional Indigenous/Yup'ik stories by non-Indigenous authors put into a Western picture-book format. Whereas many of these adaptations were accurate in their presentation of story and illustrations, others were not. As teachers further analyzed the Western notion of genre and how these were represented primarily in written form, they developed a deeper understanding of the genre represented by the Yup'ik oral stories called *quliraq* and *qanemciq*. This opened up discussions about these types of Yup'ik stories and the similarities and differences between Western notions of folktales and their oral origins. As these discussions evolved, teachers came to an understanding of how the Yup'ik oral storytelling tradition and the stories told in Yugtun were also texts that could be used in their classrooms as part of literary instruction and activities.

Semiotics of Gesture

As discussed in the Methods and Modes section, we used *yuraq* as a way to theorize and apply practical applications to the Western concept of semiotics. Briefly stated, we use the term *semiotics* to refer to multiple sign systems within which we construct meaning. This notion of constructing meaning within and across multiple sign systems, such as musical notation, visual elements (e.g., line, shape, color, texture, space), and gesture (to name a few) are at the core of the theory and practice of multiliteracies. In this theme, teachers began to recognize and apply the notion of syntax, semantics, and pragmatics, which underlie language systems, to other sign systems, such as gesture, in Yup'ik dance. In this way, the teachers made theoretical and pedagogical connections between the teaching of language and literacy and teaching the vocabulary of gesture, underscoring the lexicon and syntax of *yuraq* and other sign systems such as those used in storyknifing and multimodal interpretations like kinesthetic representation acted out in tableaux. This understanding was demonstrated as teachers participated in activities that helped teachers learn how to move from one sign system to another (transmediation) in their representing and interpretation of meaning. For example, in one activity, teachers developed a lexicon of dance gestures, which they used to storyboard a dance sequence. In developing their storyboard, they used the drawings or symbols of gestures (e.g., hand above eyes to represent looking out over the tundra) arranged in the sequence as they occurred in the dance. This technique of storyboarding was then applied to developing the sequence of poses to enact in tableaux, which interpreted a passage of a story (either written or oral). Thus, through their practical application of drawing storyboards to represent gesture as it would be performed in dance or tableaux, teachers not only developed a deeper knowledge of a particular sign system but also learned how sign systems are related and how transmediating across these sign systems could facilitate comprehension and understanding of the focus of instruction (vocabulary, storyline, concepts, etc.).

Technology as a Double-edged Tool

Although the Multiliteracies class did not include direct instruction in how to use various tools, such as GarageBand or PowerPoint, the idea was that these tools would be presented in Siekmann and Sikorski's class (see Chapter 3). Course assignments for both classes were designed so that they could overlap, allowing the teachers to focus assignments for a particular course requirement. For example, two students developed a website as part of one assignment in the Pedagogy class and incorporated an assignment from the Multiliteracies class into that website.

This theme contains two subthemes: (1) the challenges of learning how to use and manipulate the tools (e.g., podcasts, iMovie, GarageBand), and (2) the challenges of finding the right tool for a project. The first subtheme is defined by the wide range of competencies demonstrated by the teachers at the outset of the class. For example, one student had never developed a PowerPoint presentation, whereas another regularly used podcasting, GarageBand, and iMovie as instructional tools. While those teachers with greater experience felt less tension, anxiety, and resistance in the actual performance of the technological tasks, these same teachers felt tension and anxiety because they were seen as technology gurus and consequently were called on by the less experienced teachers for help.

The second subtheme deals with the challenges faced in choosing the appropriate tool for the task. In one case, a teacher chose to present an elder's story using a PowerPoint presentation. As she was working, she expressed frustration with the tool and how "it just doesn't capture the oral tradition." She struggled with how her task could be done effectively and in such a way that the authenticity of the story would not be lost. When we talked about what was important in maintaining authenticity, the idea of preserving orality emerged as the primary issue. After brainstorming how an oral story could best be presented in its oral form, the teacher chose to present the story as a podcast, instead. It was an "aha" moment for the teacher as well as for the rest of the class. Thus, within this theme, teachers initially grappled with the notion of technology as a double-edged sword, both a help and a hindrance. However, once they gained experience with manipulating the tools, they also developed a deeper understanding of which tools best fit a task.

In the following sections, we present a more detailed look into two themes—cross-cultural transmediations and pedagogy from the inside out. The sections present data from class activities, discussions, and written and presentation assignments. We chose these two themes because they illustrate how the goal of establishing a dialogue between Indigenous and Western epistemologies, methodologies, and pedagogies was carried out in actual practice. Although all the themes exhibit this dialogue to varying degrees, these two are exemplars of how it was initiated in an Indigenous voice. In other words, the practices of the teachers in the class began from the Indigenous point of view.

Cross-Cultural Transmediations

This theme involves the process of transmediation or moving between different sign systems and modes to construct and interpret meaning. An example of transmediation is beginning with an oral story, such as a *qanemciq*, and retelling it in another sign system such as *yuraq*. Furthermore, the theme also contains a distinguishing cross-cultural element because of the interaction between Indigenous and Western sign systems and modalities. An example illustrating the cross-cultural element is using a Yup'ik oral story (*qanemciq*) to create a Western genre children's picture storybook (e.g., written text and illustrations). The following vignette, which exemplifies this theme, is based on a composite of data (field notes, class presentations, written class assignments) generated in class. The vignette describes the series of instructional activities, created by a teacher participant team, that transmediate between sign systems, are multimodal, and use a multiliteracies approach.

BERRY PICKING IN FOUR MODES. The teachers were asked to develop a series of interrelated activities that could be used in their language teaching lessons. The twist was that each activity had to use a different mode (aural, oral, kinesthetic, visual, written) to develop the associated multiliteracies represented (e.g., oral story, dance, written text, visual art/drawing). Sarah Bass, Quana Holmberg, and Joanne Sundown became a team. All three teachers are fluent Yup'ik speakers. Bass teaches in a Yup'ik immersion classroom; Holmberg and Sundown teach in classrooms that use English as the primary language of instruction. However, Holmberg and Sundown also incorporate Yugtun concepts and vocabulary to explain and enhance culturally based activities. What united these teachers in this assignment was the challenge of developing activities, centered in multiliteracies, using different modalities such that they could be adapted to their teaching contexts (e.g., different language of instruction, student age levels).

The starting point was the subsistence activity of berry picking, which is practiced in all their villages. They wanted to anchor their instruction in the familiar, so that the language used (both English and Yugtun) was both relevant and taken from their students' life experience. The first activity centered on hands-on activities that used actual berries to foster talking about how to pick berries, learning Yugtun and English names of berries, sorting and storing berries, and preparing foods with berries gathered as part of their subsistence lifestyle. After building this experiential "text," Bass, Holmberg, and Sundown included a print-based text, *Berry Magic* (Huffman & Sloat 2004), a children's picture book in English that has also been translated into Yugtun. Using a book like *Berry Magic* as a read-aloud text provided a resource in English and Yugtun that could be applied in their classroom contexts. With a multimodal text like *Berry Magic*, which contains images and written language, illustrations provide visual clues to vocabulary in either Yugtun or English. The text, which is about the cultural activity of berry picking—including the process of picking, processing, and preparing foods with berries—provides a culturally relevant connection to students' lived experiences, providing another tool to help them make meaning. The instructional strategy of reading aloud, particularly picture books, was already a core instructional principle for each of the teachers because they viewed it as a practice that best provides opportunities for children to hear language and connect the oral and written word with the help of visual images to support meaning making. However, the teachers also began to view the strategy in a new way—through the lens of multiliteracies—because it added a performative dimension incorporating multimodal dramatic elements (voice inflection, gesture, facial expression, etc.).

As stated previously, transmediation is the process of how meaning is constructed and reconstructed as it moves from one sign system to another. We broaden this concept to apply to movement from one Western literary genre to another. For example, one can read a story and then compose a poem based on that story, or vice versa. The same idea can be applied to the notion of creating a children's picture book (Western literary genre) from a *qanemciq* (Yup'ik literary genre). For their second activity, thinking in terms of transmediating between Western literary genre, the teachers used *Berry Magic* to compose a poem. The final product was a poem for two voices that could be performed in a multimodal reader's theater format. There are two columns in the poem. The left side is to be read/performed by one reader and the right side by the other. When words appear on the same line and in parentheses, both readers/performers say them at the same time. The poem follows.

Berry Magic: A Poem for Two Voices
(Adapted from *Berry Magic*, by Huffman & Sloat)

Voice 1	**Voice 2**
Long ago before your grandmother's memory	
	before the salmonberries,
and raspberries,	
	before the
(cranberries)	(blueberries).
There were only	
	black crowberries
on the tundra.	
	They grew like
(dots)	(dots)
on the tops	
	of the hills.
Every fall, the old women	
	grumbled about the crowberries
"These berries	
(are so dry)	(have no taste).
	But they
picked them	
(anyway)	(anyway),
	for there had to be
(*Akutaq*)	(Eskimo ice cream),
at the fall feast.	
	And it had
to be filled with	
(BERRIES)!	(BERRIES)!

For the final activity, the teachers composed a Yup'ik dance that told the story of berry picking through movement and gesture. The dance was composed or organized into verses that contained only movement and gesture accompanied by traditional Yup'ik drumming. The movements and gestures symbolized walking on the tundra, picking berries, putting them in a basket, whipping berries into *akutaq* (commonly known as Eskimo ice cream), and finally eating the *akutaq*. The teachers wanted to focus on the notion of gesture and movement as sign/symbol and therefore did not add spoken or sung lyrics accompanied by music. The goal was to demonstrate that a dance composed solely of gesture and movement arranged in verses contained a story grammar form with syntax and structure much in the same way as written or oral story texts and could convey meaning to both participant and audience. The teachers also hoped that the movements and gestures would reinforce the vocabulary (English and Yugtun) taught in all of the preceding activities, so that students could cognitively and metacognitively transmediate between the sign systems. This cycle of transmediation, through its symbolic representation of picking berries demonstrated through dance, brought the series of activities back full circle to the initial activity of hands-on touching, identifying and sorting the berries, and making and eating *akutaq*.

Pedagogy from the Inside Out

The theme pedagogy from the inside out exemplifies the notion that there is more than one epistemological, methodological, and pedagogical framework to consider in approaches to teaching and learning. In the words of the teachers, "Yup'iit people have a rich knowledge base" and "ways of passing down knowledge and how to live a good productive life as a Yup'ik person," which have been "handed down in our stories and cultural practices for hundreds if not thousands of years" (field notes, July 9, 2009). In this theme, which is primarily based on data taken from class discussions and written drafts of rationales for thematic units, the teachers started with the Yup'ik conceptual framework of *yuuyaraq* (see the Conceptual Framework section). Drawing from their own experiences with Yup'ik knowledge, beliefs, values, and cultural practices, teachers used quotes in Yugtun from Yup'ik elders, published texts in Yugtun/English about Yup'ik knowledge and culture, and used *quliraq* and *qamenciq* (traditional stories) to develop their rationales for thematic units "from the inside" perspective. Approaching school-based instruction starting with *yuuyaraq* was in contrast to what the teachers had been taught in teacher training classes as well as in-services, which privileged the "outside" Western pedagogical perspective. This change in direction was called "from the inside out" by the Yup'ik teachers, and this practice of "from the inside out" became a trend for approaching curriculum development by all of the teachers in the class. The following excerpts are from drafts of the rationales for thematic units developed by two Yup'ik teachers—Cathy

Moses, a third-grade Yup'ik language teacher, and Carol Oulton, a first-grade Yup'ik immersion teacher—illustrating the theme of developing a pedagogy from the inside out.

Moses's Rationale (Excerpt). In the southwestern part of Alaska lies the Yup'ik region, where much of the Yup'ik population depends on fish as its main food staple. Fish diet goes back to our history for as long as time can remember. Great care and a large amount of time and energy are spent on gathering and preparing for fish. The values of gathering and storing fish include the following: respect, sharing, hard work, responsibility, helpfulness, and self-sufficiency. Another value is working together as a family or group of families. Working together usually brings a sense of mutual respect, responsibility, and self-esteem, especially when someone in the family either shows gratitude or gives praises for the work. As Marie Nichols (Tennant & Bitar 1981, p. 110), a Yup'ik elder from Kasigluk, states: "Qalarut'lall-ruitkut wangkuta ayagyuallemteni, neqa kiingan yugmun yuutekni-luku. Kiigngan angniutnguniluku, quuyurnitnguniluku, allaniu-rutnguniluki, cali-llu-gguq tungayangqerrutnguluni." Translated as "When we were young they used to tell us that food is the only thing that kept a person going, the only reason for happiness, the only reason for smiling, the only thing to offer a guest, and the only reason one had relatives."

If we stop and think about the wise words of this elder, we come to realize that our daily lives are, in fact, centered on our main diet, fish. It's like a hidden drive that connects all the people who live amongst us. The part about having relatives is an important concept, because it's one that makes society what it is. Fish is like glue that connects the whole community, both in a social sense and wellness of, as well as on the economical point of view. There's also a Yup'ik saying that says, no matter how poor one may be, possession-wise, they are considered "rich" as long as they have fish to eat. Our children and students need to know these Yup'ik ideas and beliefs handed down from previous generations because they help us to think of others in a respectful manner as well as the community as a whole. The center of our relationship, like a grass basket, is woven around daily subsistence-related activities and one of these is fishing.

Oulton's Rationale (Excerpt). Another important sociocultural practice of our ancestors is the use of moss. It is a plant used as a bottom

> and top layer for stink heads, which were fermented in pits during the summer. There are some families who continue to practice fermenting salmon heads using the same implementation. In our historical cultural context, the moss was used for diapers, menstrual periods, and preparing food. Mary Black (Tennant & Bitar 1981, p. 124) told a story of how moss was used: "Passiluki uqurrarmek avuqaqluki, mermek-llu avuurluki. Akuquraami amlleriluni, tan'gerpagnek-llu qivirluku tauna. Tuaten-llu cali ner'aqluku. Tuamta-llu, pavani nunapignek avurnaurtut urunek." Mary said they used to crush moss and slowly added water and seal oil in small quantities. The moss expanded, and blackberries were added. This is how they consumed it. In addition, moss was a tool for sealing the kayak seams. First, it had to be hung, dried, soaked in seal oil, rolled, and stowed until it became rotten and sticky. From doing this, the kayak did not leak.
>
> Even though Mary tells a short story, it is an example of an epistemological theory. . . . Mary has the knowledge from observing her ancestors in the act of how the moss was used. At the time of her recording, there were changes in the area, but she did not leave behind the knowledge that she learned. She brought the knowledge from present to past. From that, she connects what she knows of the moss into her surroundings during that time.
>
> Today, much of the knowledge of gathering plants is written in anthropology books, and not many families practice gathering plants. Before this history becomes just a story, lessons on gathering plants should be taught in our schools. This is the importance of why schools need to implement multiliteracies into their curriculum. As Martin (2008) says in her article multiliteracies incorporate the visual, spatial, gestural, linguistics, and audio learning. As language teachers, we need to think about these modes in planning our curriculum.

This trend of using elders' cultural knowledge as a theoretical framework and the inclusion of Yup'ik epistemology, methodology, and pedagogy for developing their units and lessons within the units was evident in all of the class participants' writing assignments and became an expected and accepted norm. Yup'ik teachers felt free to include the written transcriptions of oral stories and teachings by Yup'ik elders because they viewed these as academic theoretical and methodological "texts" by Indigenous scholars. In the words of one student: "This should be a guiding principle for *all* teachers, especially for those of us who are non-Native. We can't just rely only on Western theories and concepts and teaching methods. And for new non-Native teachers to the village, we have to help them be open to learn how to access and use Yup'ik cultural principles to guide their instruction" (student journal).

As previously stated, creating a dialogue between Indigenous/Yup'ik and Western theories, epistemologies, methodologies, and pedagogies was a primary goal as the conceptual basis for course content and as the method for class implementation. What proved most compelling was how this dialogue did not always initiate from a Western perspective. In the case of the examples explicating the themes of cross-cultural transmediation and pedagogy from the inside out, the dialogue was initiated by an Indigenous/Yup'ik voice. This was also illustrated in our analysis related to the conceptual framework for the class (see Table 4.2). In both themes, the starting point for the teachers was Yup'ik epistemology and Yup'ik pedagogy based in cultural knowledge and the traditional ways of passing that knowledge onto other generations. In the vignette exemplifying the cross-cultural transmediation theme, the teachers began their development of instructional activities with the traditional subsistence practice of berry picking, which has its theoretical and methodological base in *yuuyaraq*. In the more theoretically focused pedagogy from the inside out theme, the teachers started with *yuuyaraq* to frame the content and instructional strategies for their thematic units.

Even in those themes in which the Western voice of theory and methodology was the initiator (e.g., consonance/dissonance in multimodal genre, semiotics of gesture, technology as a double-edged tool), a dialogue with Indigenous/Yup'ik epistemology, theory, and practice still emerged. Opening up a dialogue between Indigenous/Yup'ik and Western theories and methodologies also opened a space that allowed Indigenous/Yup'ik voices equity in conversations about educational theories and practices. Thus, operating within this third space allowed the teachers (both Yup'ik and non-Native) to create a new kind of pedagogy that combined both Yup'ik and Western knowledge systems and instructional methodologies.

Reflections on Practice

At the end of every instructional time period like the summer session, like most other teachers who have just completed teaching a class, we took time to debrief and reflect on how our goals and aspirations for the class compared with actual practices. What were the successes, the challenges, and the changes that needed to happen before the next course offering? Part of our analytical process was to evaluate our instructional practice to determine the overall strengths and challenges that emerged over the course of the class. By engaging in this reflexive process we hoped we could continue the dialogue by reframing in theory and practice what it means to become a literate person able to make meaning in a multilingual, multicultural, and multimodal world. In the following sections, we outline what we determined as the strengths and challenges of the class as well as our next steps.

Strengths

An overarching strength was the practical application of establishing a dialogue between the Indigenous and Western epistemologies, theories, and methodologies that formed the conceptual foundation and framed the implementation of the class. This dialogic conceptual framework, which was developed from input and contributions from all participants, had its beginnings prior to the class in regular GRC meetings. Building a theoretical framework continued throughout the summer session and was strengthened as teachers put these theories into practice. In partnership with the development of the dialogic conceptual framework, instruction was also carried out as a dialogue between John and Parker Webster, which was a natural extension of how they approached their collaborative research. Probably the greatest strength, which was an outgrowth of all these dialogic practices, was the emergence of the Indigenous voice as initiator of the dialogue.

Challenges

Of course, one of the biggest challenges is time. The summer session lasted just under four weeks, and teachers were involved in taking two classes—ours and a curriculum development class taught by Siekmann and Sikorski (see Chapter 3 for a complete discussion). While instructors of both classes planned course assignments that could overlap (e.g., learning teachnology tools by completing tasks for Siekmann and Sikorski could also be framed as part of a lesson for the multiliteracies thematic unit assignment), the steep learning curve experienced in gaining technological skills and learning new content in a three-week period was a challenge for teachers and instructors alike. As illustrated in a prior example, some teachers took more time to understand the technological tool well enough to match the task to the tool. This lack of time also impeded more in-depth explorations into transmediations between Yup'ik modalities (e.g., dancing, storyknifing, storytelling) as well as similar modalities across Alaska Native groups (e.g., Athabascan, Inupiaq, Tlingit).

Perhaps the greatest challenge is the need for systemic changes in schooling and school curriculum. Although there have been great strides in curriculum development in Alaska's bush/village school districts to incorporate culturally based knowledge and subsistence-based activities, these are most often regarded as supplementary materials to support prescriptive and standardized reading or math curricula produced by large, commercial publishing houses. Likewise, culturally based modes of expression and interpretation of knowledge, such as those embodied in multiliteracies, have been given more attention in curriculum development, particularly in schools with predominantly Alaska Native student populations (e.g., bush/village schools and some urban charter schools). However, because state standardized tests privilege the linguistic sign system and modes (e.g., reading, writing), the notion of expressing and interpreting knowledge in other modalities is not regarded as a valid assessment of learning.

Next Steps

In our view, there is great need for a systemic change in curriculum development with instruction and assessment that moves away from predominantly linguistic modes to include multiliteracies and multimodalities. At the time of writing this chapter, a consortium of teachers, composed of some of the participants in the SLATE program, engaged in creating curriculum materials in the heritage language and using multiliteracies and multimodalities in instruction and assessment (see Siekmann and Sikorski, Chapter 3 and Epilogue of this volume, as well as Marlow & Siekmann forthcoming). This curriculum project represents first steps toward enacting systemic change through (1) organizing a professional network for advocacy for curriculum and assessment reform at the district and state levels, and (2) ongoing development of curriculum materials in the heritage language, using cultural activities that incorporate multiliteracies and multimodalities. However, while these are giant steps in the right direction, systemic change also must involve changes in district and state policies regarding heritage language maintenance and revitalization (see

Chapter 6), as well as district and statewide assessment policies and practices (see Chapter 5). SLATE, through its master's degree program, opened leadership pathways for the teachers involved. These kinds of opportunities must be sustained for real systemic change to occur.

Notes

1. The Zone of Proximal Development, as defined by Vygotsky (1978), is the distance between the actual development level as determined by independent problem solving and the level of potential development as determined through problem solving under adult guidance or in collaboration with more capable peers. In other words, within the ZPD is the knowledge that the learner does not yet understand but has the ability to learn, to grasp what is just out of her reach with help from a more knowledgeable adult or peer.

2. In a directive scaffolding model, the teacher's goal is to transmit knowledge to the student. In this model, the conversational pattern, described by Cazden (1988) as Initiation-Response-Evaluation, is teacher-driven: the teacher asks a question that has a predetermined answer, the student responds, and the teacher evaluates the answer for the correct response. In a supportive scaffolding model, the conversational pattern may include explicit modeling or direct explanation by the teacher, but it also invites students to participate in the conversation through student-driven exploration, which is supported by the teacher's verification or challenging of students' understanding without providing the "answer" (Gallas 1995; Wilkinson & Siliman 2000).

3. *Qanemciq* is a story that originated in "distant time" (Wiget 1985)—a period marked by creative flux in which characters can be animal and human, both speak the same language, and can transform at will—and it has the stamp and authority of collective tradition and authorship. Raven as creator is one kind of *qanemciq*. *Quliraq* is a type of narrative about a particular person or event, either in present or historic times. According to Annie Blue, elder and storyteller from Togiak, *quliraq* can often become *qanemciq* over a period of time.

CHAPTER FIVE

Teachers Drawing on the Power of Place to Indigenize Assessment

Marilee Coles-Ritchie and Walkie Charles

This chapter focuses on data generated in the summer intensive course "Assessment for the Second Language Classroom." The course focused on theories of assessment, particularly pressing issues for K–12 teachers in the era of No Child Left Behind (NCLB), and practical development and implementation of authentic assessments based on Indigenous community resources. Using data collected through student and teacher reflections, field notes from the classroom, and portfolios, we demonstrate how the teachers combined elements of funds of knowledge (Gonzalez, Moll, & Amanti 2005) and authentic assessment (O'Malley & Pierce 1996) to reconstruct ways of assessing students' language development in Yugtun and English based on Indigenous community practices. This chapter illustrates how teachers indigenized assessment by "drawing on the power of their place" (Deloria & Wildcat 2001) to align assessments to the values, symbols, and practices of their communities. During the course, teachers collaboratively developed action plans to counter the dominant national practice, which heavily emphasized standardized tests over locally constructed assessments (Abedi 2004; Gutierrez et al. 2002; Karp 2003).

The data for this research were collected and analyzed by Marilee Coles-Ritchie, a non-Yup'ik faculty member, and Walkie Charles, a Yup'ik doctoral student/faculty member, who coconstructed and cotaught the course. Following our conceptional framework and research design,, we explore and analyze four themes that emerged from the data. We then offer implications of the study and questions for further research.

Conceptual Framework

To understand the context of this study, we draw on three main conceptual frameworks: Indigenous knowledge systems, funds of knowledge, and community of learners. We designed the course structure and content to reflect the strengths and backgrounds of the teachers (all women, primarily Yup'ik) taking the course and the students they teach in the Yup'ik region of Alaska. To achieve this, we drew heavily on the theory of Indigenous knowledge systems for education (Barnhardt & Kawagley 2005; Battiste 2002; Cajete 2008; Deloria & Wildcat 2001; Lomawaima & McCarty 2006; McCarty & Watahomigie 1999). Scholars have developed this framework using research demonstrating the value of Indigenous educators making educational institutions their own by actively "indigenizing" them. In other words, the "people historically and culturally connected to places can and do draw on power located in those places" (Deloria & Wildcat, p. 31). Marie Battiste (2002) adds that these knowledge systems are dynamic, embedded in context, and derived from local practices of individuals and communities. In our course, we tried to create spaces and projects where the teachers could draw from their collective resources to build assessment that was validated in Yup'ik context and history.

We used strategies from funds of knowledge research that complemented the Indigenous systems framework to strengthen the course. Norma Gonzalez, Luis C. Moll, and Cathy Amanti (2005) describe funds of knowledge as a way of conceptualizing households as repositories of knowledge that are borne out of social networks. These funds of knowledge can be activated by teachers in classrooms as they develop curriculum to draw on these dynamic pedagogical resources. As university instructors, we encouraged teachers to draw on their long-standing Yup'ik social network's funds of knowledge when responding to the course assignments. Also, the teachers were invited to apply the funds of knowledge tools when developing assessments for their classrooms. These assessments were grounded in their students' funds of knowledge, which might combine traditional Yup'ik understanding and knowledge with new technologies and ways of thinking adapted to changes in the environment.

Finally, we attempted to create a community of learners (Lave & Wegner 1991) committed to working together to construct knowledge and learn from one another as a community of practice. We felt that all members of the class (K–12 teachers and university faculty) were integral to understanding the course content. Each member brought funds of knowledge sometimes not recognized in their educational communities; therefore, they needed to have voice and be heard by the other members of the class. In addition, the goals of the class were focused on the assessment needs of the larger community, not only on knowledge gained by individual members of the class.

We drew on all of these frameworks in conducting this teacher action research. The foundation of teacher action research is to develop understanding of how adaptation and change in action and practice can collectively benefit a community of practitioners (McNiff & Whitehead 2006; Mills 2003). In our study, we were attempting to understand not just our own practice but also how this community of teacher researchers was going to respond to the climate of high-stakes testing in a critical way (Karp 2003). At this time the NCLB mandate required all schools be accountable by showing growth on standardized tests. These tests were particularly problematic in the Yup'ik region because they were given in English even if the students were enrolled in Yup'ik immersion schools. Therefore, we combined ideas from Bill Atweh, Stephen Kemmis, and Patricia Weeks (1998), Geoffrey E. Mills (2003), and David H. Tripp (1990) to create a theory for our research, which we call critical teacher action research (CTAR). CTAR applies critical theory to teacher action research. We explain how we use CTAR in our research design section.

Research Design

Two central research questions emerged to guide this study:

- How can we (non-Yup'ik assistant professor and Yup'ik non–tenure-track faculty member and doctoral candidate) create a course for in-service teachers working in rural southwestern Alaska that includes concepts and strategies for indigenizing assessment in a high-stakes testing environment?
- What are the relevant themes surrounding assessment in the K–12 environment for Yup'ik immersion and English language development teachers in rural Alaska?

This study used a variety of qualitative data collection approaches, including teacher classroom dialogue, researchers' journals and observation notes, memos of classroom and course planning activities, teachers' academic work (reflective quizzes, discussion facilitator notes, assessment rubrics and checklists, portfolio artifacts, and reflections), teachers' evaluations of the course, and informal interviews in person and by email. In this design, the researchers became facilitators as the teachers shared their experiences in the language classroom, their philosophies about assessment, and their emergent knowledge about assessment theory. The cooperative learning structure, with the goal of creating a community of learners, involved everyone. In this section, we share the data-collection process, including our use of CTAR methods, a profile of the participants, and how we analyzed our data.

Data Collection and Procedures

Based on CTAR, we used qualitative case study methods; together we read and reread the data, constructed themes, and coded the data for those emerging themes. We describe the elements of our study that are supported by the CTAR framework: participation, direction, consciousness, constraints, and outcomes (Tripp 1990).

First, participation of a group of teachers with similar goals and working contexts contributes to the effectiveness of CTAR. In our study, all the teachers worked in southwestern Alaska, and all worked primarily with Yup'ik children. Both instructors were interested in guiding the teachers in developing authentic and culturally appropriate assessments based in their Indigenous knowledge systems and to create an atmosphere in which they could develop counter-Discourse to challenge the standardized testing climate. We use James Paul Gee's (1992) definition of Discourse: "A Discourse is a socially accepted association among ways of using language, of thinking, feeling, believing, valuing, and of acting that can be used to identify oneself as a member of a socially meaningful group or 'social network' or to signal (that one is playing) a socially meaningful role" (p. 143). Discourses circulate until they become "normal" or "natural."

Second, CTAR needs to have direction. By this, we mean the research has a purpose to improve a certain context. In this action research study, our goals for the course gave direction for the project. Because both a Yup'ik doctoral candidate and a non-Yup'ik faculty member constructed the course syllabus and design, insider/outsider knowledge contributed to the overall goals to include a space for the teachers to help guide the further direction of the project. To examine the goals of the course, we revisited the syllabus and student surveys that indicated the teachers' expectations.

Third, consciousness needs to be explored. What were the participants' embedded values concerning aspirations, ideologies, practices, and discourses about assessment? Through this aspect of CTAR, all of the participants reflected about their own assessment practices and those they read about and studied during the course. This reflection occurred through class discussion, on reflective quizzes, and in portfolio reflections.

Fourth, CTAR requires that the researcher determine the constraints of their project. Barney Glaser and Anselm Strauss (1967) call these material (numbers of students, time, working space) and conceptual features (performance, acceptable community practices). In our study, material features included a short time (intensive four-week summer course) for exploring the issues, discussing them, and developing the appropriate assessments. Conceptual features included the difficulty of fighting the state's mandated assessments once the teachers were back in their schools. This was especially challenging because the teachers would no longer have the emotional and physical support of the community we developed.

Finally, outcomes are an important aspect of CTAR. By using CTAR, we were committed to develop practices that would be instrumental in pushing against current socially unjust practices. It involves initiating action that can help improve the school practices that disadvantage certain groups of students. In our project, the outcome goal was for the teachers in the course, who had a deep understanding of local practices and community knowledge, to create assessments that would better demonstrate the educational growth of their students. In addition, another desired outcome was equipping the teachers to be able to confront some of the national/community Discourse (Gee 1992) that emphasized standardized tests with new Discourse that included Yup'ik community values.

Profile of the Participants

The participants in this study (see also Chapter 1) included six Yup'ik teachers and one non-Yup'ik teacher, all women. All were part of either the Assessment or the Policy and Planning Graduate Research Collaborative (GRC), two of four subgroups of the federally funded Second Language Acquisition Teacher Education (SLATE) program. They were selected because they were all enrolled in the course and a part of the grant. In the study, the students in the class were called "teachers" or "teacher participants" as they took on this role in the course activities (see Table 5.1). In addition, the authors of this chapter (Coles-Ritchie and Charles) were participants in the study as the course instructors.

Table 5.1. Teacher Participants in Study

Teacher Participants	*Gender*	*Employment in the School*	*Language of Instruction*	*Ethnic Identity*
Green	Female	Elementary teacher	English	Yup'ik Eskimo
Hendrickson	Female	Elementary teacher	English	Kass'aq (Caucasian)
Amos-Andrew	Female	Elementary teacher	Yugtun	Yup'ik Eskimo
Nicholai	Female	District Yup'ik curriculum specialist	Yugtun	Yup'ik Eskimo
Michael	Female	Elementary teacher	Yugtun	Yup'ik Eskimo
Hoffman	Female	Elementary teacher	English	Yup'ik Eskimo/Hispanic
Bond	Female	Secondary teacher	English	Yup'ik Eskimo

The Process: A Collaborative Approach

As coinstructors, we jointly designed the course "Assessment for the Second Language Classroom." Coles-Ritchie took the lead on the course design and content because she had taught similar courses many times before, and Charles was physically away teaching in a Yup'ik immersion program in rural Alaska. By distance, Charles was consulted for appropriate articles and task designs. The course met during the summer during a four-week period, every other day, for six hours each session. We adopted a course design that focused on a community of learners approach.

Table 5.2. Instructor Participants in the Study

Instructor Participants	*Gender*	*Background Information*	*Language of Instruction*	*Ethnic Identity*
Coles-Ritchie	Female	Assistant professor, 10 years' university teaching experience, 10 years in K–12 classrooms	English	Kass'aq (Caucasian)
Charles	Male	Faculty member, 8 years' university language teaching experience, 10 years in K–12 classrooms	English and Yugtun	Yup'ik Eskimo

We attempted to create this community of learners by physically setting up the classroom desks in a complete circle so that everyone could see everyone else's face. Before the first session, we wrote the first objective, "begin to build classroom community," on the board. To begin this process, we started the session by asking the teachers to share a story that represented something about them. As instructors, we broke the ice by sharing stories ourselves. Coles-Ritchie told a story of climbing Mount Kenya with a group of women (and without porters), and Charles shared a traumatic tale of open-heart surgery. Each class member, in random order, shared a story. Most involved experiences with subsistence living or life in their Yup'ik villages. One told of her first successful hunting trip and another about how the past summer she had moved from the observer/learner role for cutting fish to the one who led by example.[1] Many were stories of learning from elders and teaching that knowledge to others. During this opening session, we laughed a lot, and even though the students had all known each other for at least a year or more, they said they learned new dimensions of the character of their classmates. This open sharing, where we were all equally vulnerable, set the stage for building a community of trust, respect, interaction, and common goals.

Before every class session, the instructors held a planning session to share conversations each of us had with students in or outside of class, to decide on the tasks for the next day and to assess whether we needed a new direction. We reviewed the previous session's highlights and ways we could improve the session by trying different activities, changing groups, or using Yup'ik as the language of instruction for the Yup'ik language speakers.

Teachers were invited to actively participate in every session. Table 5.3 lists the activities they participated in during the class and their purpose. We refer to some of these activities in the analysis of themes that emerged.

We designed these activities so that the students would take ownership of the material and begin to direct the learning in the class.

Developing a Classroom Community

We began each session by displaying on a large projector screen a set of objectives and a list of class activities written by the instructors and the teachers, who were facilitating the discussion on the assigned reading for that class period. These involved a variety of student-centered (or teacher-centered in this case as the participants are referred to as teachers) and instructor-led activities. The teachers were actively involved and account-

Table 5.3. Class Activities and Purpose

Class Activity	*Purpose*
Pair/share	• Discuss literature's main concepts • Make personal connections with the readings
Small group	• Discuss open-ended provocation questions • Construct authentic assessments • Connect assessment theory to Indigenous knowledge systems
Teacher facilitator discussions	• Create meaning from assessment theory • Relate course readings to Yup'ik ways of knowing • Scaffold reading for peers
Annotated bibliography	• Demonstrate ability to critique and summarize assessment literature • Reflect on language assessment literature and connect it to a local context
Personal reflections	• Connect readings to personal experience • Express ideas in Yup'ik
Portfolio creation	• Demonstrate a model of assessment • Connect course content to local context • Reflect on language assessment theory • Create authentic assessment for use in local context

able in every class session. Because of the number of small group and pair activities, teachers had numerous opportunities to share their insights and opinions. This structure helped facilitate the themes that developed during the four-week session and beyond.

The essence of classroom community was shared in a reflection by Atan (Veronica) Michael. She wrote, "Kiimetengnaqluta kiimesqualuta pisciigataput taugaam ikayuqutenganqluta. Tua-i-tang yuuyararput" (We cannot do this alone, attempting to do this by ourselves, but as a community. This is the Yup'ik way of living). This reflection was written toward the end of the course, when the class had established itself as a community of learners in which knowledge was shared among the group members. Vine Deloria Jr. and Daniel R. Wildcat (2001) address the need to change the complete framework of education from one that is individualized to the collective. In their introduction, Wildcat explains: "It is critical to understand that Deloria's essays are not primarily about raising standards or improving test scores, rather they constitute a reasonable call to consider the advantages of building an educational practice on a foundation of American Indian metaphysics that 'is a unified world view acknowledging a complex totality in the world' " (p. 9). Within our class of primarily Yup'ik teachers, developing a community in which each person could contribute to the goals of the class was critical. We designed the course to allow for continual contribution and collaboration to meet the core objectives. These activities included a pair of teachers acting as discussion facilitators, teacher selection of assessment research, portfolio development, and many group activities that allowed for collaborative development of assessments.

To illustrate how the community of learners began to develop and open up spaces for this contribution, we share one of the course assignments, "discussion facilitator." At the beginning of the course, we shared a list of assigned articles. In pairs, teachers signed up for an article of interest. As codiscussion facilitators, they were responsible for leading the discussion of a reading for one twenty- to thirty-minute period. The discussion facilitator gave a brief synopsis of the reading and prepared a short set of open-ended discussion questions or activities to stimulate discussion and clear up any questions about the reading. The teachers were responsible for guiding the discussion and connecting it to their local ways of knowing.

As the teachers directed the course, a shift occurred as class members began looking to one another for answers and more questions rather than directing them just to the instructors. They began to rely on each other and bond as a class. In reflective writing, students expressed ideas in the plural: "We are a strong and proud people." "I think the move for our class is to eventually do just that." "This is where the poster that was created for the whole class comes in!" "We are making our voices heard through their system." Through these statements, the teachers illustrated their bond as a class community and their desire to move ideas forward as a collective. They showed that they trusted and respected one another through interaction and construction of the course. As Marilyn Cochran-Smith and Susan L. Lytle (1993) write, "In every classroom where teachers are learners and all learners are teachers, there is a radical but quiet kind of school reform in process" (p. 101). This reform began with the development of this community of learners.

Discussion and Findings

This course provided a platform for teachers to contribute to the goals of the course. Sharing a wealth of knowledge about the values and contributions of their home communities, they developed critical Indigenous assessments in a time when standardized assessments dominated the public school community. Through these conversations and shared construction of assessment, they developed a bond as a community of learners. In this section we explore the following themes that emerged from our research, including (1) recontextualizing concepts to reflect Indigenous local practices, (2) developing ways to challenge dominant standardized assessment practices, and (3) developing authentic assessment measures using community funds of knowledge.

Recontextualizing Concepts to Reflect Indigenous Local Practices

As we began to explore the core concepts of assessment, many more questions arose. At times, the teachers were confused with the textbook explanations. As a fluent Yup'ik speaker, Charles opened the door for the teachers to express themselves in Yugtun at any time. Coles-Ritchie assured them that she wanted them to use Yup'ik even though she would not understand. Many times the teachers expressed feeling safe and comfortable explaining exactly the way the words were heard from an elder or a parent in Yugtun. Translation was unnecessary, which allowed the "sacredness" of the Yup'ik quote or comment to stand. Coles-Ritchie made it a point not to ask for translation and relied on Charles to make the connections in these situations. Two other students, a white teacher and a Yup'ik Eskimo who didn't speak Yugtun, also respected the conversations in Yugtun.

Often, Charles was able to reconstruct an academic concept in Yugtun so that the teachers would better understand the meaning. For example, in one class session we were discussing the Vygotskian-based practice of dynamic assessment, a dialogic approach to assessment that demonstrates how an individual's responsiveness to assistance is indicative of his or her future performance (Poehner & Lantolf 2005). As we were studying this concept, which was complicated in beginning stages, a teacher said, "Oh, they don't always get it the first time around so I need to *qaruteq* [guide, counsel, and encourage] them. Each time they experienced this, they learn from their previous mistakes. Each experience contributes to continued learning. Dynamic assessment is to *qaruteq* them or guide them along" (teacher reflection).

Charles used a Yup'ik term, *qaruyun*, as a way of showing support and guidance to the teachers using this new concept in the classroom, just as a parent or caretaker in a Yup'ik home would guide, counsel, and encourage a child learning a new task or experience. Many teachers nodded their heads to show understanding as this Yup'ik expression was used to make sense of an academic concept.

Another example illustrating the idea of reconceptualizing concepts to reflect local Indigenous practices came from a teacher responding to the article "Creating a Third Space for Authentic Biculturalism" (Lipka, Sharp, Adams, & Sharp 2007) as part of an annotations assignment. She wrote: "I am a strong believer in third space. I know our children can make the best of two worlds especially when a child is led to make connections with an experienced [Yup'ik] teacher who can guide them. Yup'ik knowledge can be connected to parts of content in English" (teacher reflection). By examining these powerful words through the frameworks of Indigenous knowledge systems, we see how this teacher made the academic concept fit her lived practices. As a person historically and culturally connected to a Yup'ik community, she was drawing on the power located in that place to make connections for students in a dynamic way (Deloria 1991). These teachers were practicing what Beatrice Medicine called for specifically: "more research [by Indigenous scholars] in [bilingual-bicultural education] and for *reporting back* to communities so that they could use research to devise academically sound education programs that promoted local languages and cultures" (Deyhle & McCarty 2007, p. 214). Numerous examples during the course illustrated the way students were drawing on local practice and language to make sense of new content. The way they made sense of new content created "a new center," as described by Bryan McKinley Jones Brayboy and Emma Maughan (2009), in which Western and Indigenous knowledges complement each other through providing educational spaces to connect the ideas.

Developing Ways to Challenge Dominant Standardized Assessment Practices

While exercising the power that comes from drawing on the community funds of knowledge rooted in Indigenous knowledge systems, the teachers also experienced frustration as they recognized the ways that they had changed their teaching practice to fit the current standardized assessments. They realized that they, too, were "teaching to the test," as described in many of the readings. Two teachers volunteered to facilitate a discussion on a required reading, "Making Assessment Practices Valid for Indigenous American Students" (Nelson-Barber & Trumbull 2007). During that class session, they focused on the following excerpt from the article: "The unfortunate outcome of the NCLB legislation may well be that educators of Native students move further away from culturally congruent curriculum, instruction and assessment rather than increasing their use—despite all the evidence of their value and despite the intent of Executive Orders 13096 (1998) and 13270 (2002)" (Nelson-Barber & Trumbull 2007, p. 134). The idea that teachers were moving away from "culturally congruent" curriculum and teaching practice because of NCLB provoked a heated discussion and intense emotion. At least one teacher began to cry openly. We sat silent with our thoughts for at least five minutes. Later in the day, many teachers expressed their frustration at falling into the "trap" of standardized assessments. They told stories of moving away from practices that they knew were more beneficial for their Indigenous students so that they could meet the requirements of the standardized tests. These expressions were later written in their reflections. Every class member in the course expressed thoughts concerning teaching practice geared toward standardized testing. A few examples of these statements are shared below:

> Our answers to raising test scores in the educational system are right in the heart of our people, in our culture and in our language, and yet we try so hard to please others, we forget our own culture and language. (teacher reflection)

> I'm in awe and angry knowing what I have done to my students. There were points in my teaching career that I thought, "Okay, how best can I teach [to the test]?" When all the while, I should have been wondering further, "Why does this not look right?" (teacher reflection)

> I agree that testing has become the official driving force to reform education. In our school, we have placed so much emphasis on passing the standardized tests. We have failed to make AYP [Adequate Yearly Progress] for seven years now. Every principal we have had has stressed over and over again that we need to pass the test. Every time we fail meeting the requirements, we are made to feel that we are not good teachers. (teacher reflection)

After the teachers grieved, they decided they wanted to do something to "fight back on the NCLB." As a class, we developed a handout titled "The

Choice to Raise a Child" (Figure 5.1). The goal was to create something that the teachers could give to parents who were worried that placing their children in Yup'ik immersion programs would lower their test scores. In the middle of the handout was a photo of Yup'ik children playing outside.

During this session, the class members worked in collaboration as a

The Choice to Raise a Child

Do you want to raise your child with high test scores?	*Do you want your child to learn Yugtun & Yugtun Values?*
SBAs, Reading, Writing, Math Annual Report Benchmark completion Test driven instruction (Tests determine the lessons) Skill & Drill Weaknesses Highlighted Focus is on what your child CAN'T do Western dominated views California, Texas Colonial Views emphasized English prioritized Funds go to testing companies Driven by economic growth (greed) Competitive Individualistic Structured	Culturally relevant curriculum Authentic Assessments Continuous Reports Multiple Reports Student-centered Elders and Community Involvement Funds of Knowledge Child's interests explored Strengths Highlighted Focus is on what child CAN do Based on local environment/knowledge Native knowledge emphasized YUUYARAQ Funds stay in the community YUGTUN VALUES Collaborative Holistic

LING 612: Assessment
Project SLATE, Summer - 2008

Figure 5.1. The choice to raise a child (source: Coles-Ritchie & Charles 2011)

community of learners, drawing on their Yup'ik knowledge and values to construct a material artifact that could be used against this testing system, which they believed was interfering with practices that would better serve their students. The idea of fighting against standardized tests was also mirrored in their reflective writing. One teacher wrote: "It's okay to question the system after all; we can do better for our students. Even us, the teachers, gloat to an extent that yes, our students are passing the tests and this should be a reminder to us to 'keep it real.' We need to continue to keep our school as real as possible" (teacher reflection). Stating that the teachers needed to "keep it real" was a way of saying that they needed to reflect the local Indigenous practices and knowledge, draw on the power in their places, and not fall into the trap of moving away from Native ways of knowing to prepare students for the test.

After reading Angela Cavender Wilson's (2004) chapter on decolonization and the recovery of Indigenous knowledge, one of the teachers wrote this powerful reflection:

> This article is an excellent reference in my research on parental choice and the whole idea behind manufactured consent and the negative impact of colonization and how it has affected the way that we think about our culture and schools. It is profound to think about how we as Indigenous peoples have been brainwashed into believing that the Western way of thinking is the best way if we want to be successful. I enjoyed reading Wilson's perspective, because it helps me understand what my ancestors went through, as well as my own mother when she was sent to boarding school. It helps me clarify and identify the reasoning behind critical events that occurred in our family history. It also reminds me of the damage that was done to our Native people, language, and culture. Wilson is a strong advocate to get our language, culture and voice back. I embrace her strong message of becoming scholars so that we can be the speakers and voices of our people. I believe that is what this SLATE program is all about, and look forward to the day where more Native people will begin to make a stronger commitment in passing on traditional knowledge and language to their children. (teacher reflection)

This teacher writes from a "place" she knows well—the power of family history, home practices, language use, and the long-term effects of colonization. When she reflects on this article, she does so from a deep knowledge of how Indigenous people adapt and learn from their contexts. She also shows her frustration at what she calls "being brainwashed" into thinking that a Western way of learning is most effective. By acknowledging Wilson as "a strong advocate to get our language, culture and voice back" she links back to the importance of committing local Indigenous people into the education system. She is recognizing herself as an advocate and realizing that more Indigenous advocates are needed.

In this section, the "critical" part of action research is demonstrated when a group of people fight against the dominant system, which is negatively impacting their local practices. The students collectively developed a handout to advocate for Indigenous language programs that reflect a holistic and collaborative way of learning rooted in Yup'ik values of respect and sharing. They also reflected on ways to fight against standardized tests by first recognizing that they were complicit in molding their teaching to fit the test's goals, rather than relying on their own knowledge of effective teaching practice for the community. They shared the importance of challenging this system by drawing on their funds of knowledge and Indigenous knowledge systems.

Developing Authentic Assessment Measures Using Community Funds of Knowledge

One of the primary goals of the class was for teachers to create authentic assessments (O'Malley & Pierce 1996) based on their community's funds of knowledge. By *authentic assessments*, we mean multiple forms of assessment that reflect student learning, achievement, perspectives, and ideologies. Examples include performance, portfolios, and student/peer self-assessment that align with real-world tasks. To accomplish this goal, the teachers were involved in many small group activities in which we provided current Alaska state standards or curriculum goals. With these curriculum goals, the teachers developed a way to assess that goal by developing a culturally congruent assessment. They often started with a rubric or checklist example from the textbook, which they would adapt to fit resources or cultural artifacts familiar to the students.

During one class session, Renee Green shared a rubric she had created for teachers to use when evaluating a child's participation in a group project. Everyone got excited because the rubric was created with the image of a Yup'ik dance drum. It was designed to demonstrate a child's participation in a group project. It included the drum, handle, and drumstick. In the middle she wrote "good" participation. It included the drum with the handle but no stick. She typed "fair" participation on the other end. It included only the circle of the drum but no stick or handle. She explained, "In the back of my mind I am trying to make things culturally relevant for my students. Unlike rubrics that are made with images of hamburgers or ice cream cones, drums represent celebrations for us." Green's drum also included specific criteria for the task. The statements included: "My partner was on task. My partner was a big asset to the assignment. My partner allowed others to give their ideas. My partner worked well with everyone on the team." These criteria reflected Yup'ik values of collaboration and collective project building.

Another teacher shared the following idea: "My biggest challenge is to teach kids to persuade and to evaluate. One way the students could be engaged in a local problem is to investigate the destruction of egg-hunting grounds. I would have the students work together in groups to come up with a list of arguments in favor of keeping four-wheelers off the land. I could videotape each group with their information to make it look like a commercial. They would be assessed based on a rubric" (Teacher reflection). These activities allowed them to learn from one another within the classroom community and also encouraged them to draw from their Indigenous knowledge and resources. One teacher wrote, "Rather than devaluing our cultural knowledge and keeping it out of the classrooms, we have found ways to integrate it into the curriculum and at the same time get the students to show what they know. The knowledge I have gained just makes me upset because there are teachers in my village who don't make an effort to teach relevant units. Some teachers who are from the outside teach the students about farm animals and space, which just goes to show they have no idea about what works for us" (teacher reflection). This reflection illustrates the power and strength that come from the community's funds of knowledge. She is advocating the use of cultural knowledge in the classroom and recognizing that her Indigenous knowledge "works" for the students. She is also acknowledging the reason that it is difficult sometimes for those from "outside," or someone from the "lower forty-eight" (referring to the contiguous United States), to teach in a way that reflects local knowledge. Interestingly, one of the teachers was from the outside, and we wondered at times whether she felt comfortable with parts of the discussion that clearly emphasized strengths of the Yup'ik teachers. As a person committed to the village where she had taught for nearly four years, she told Coles-Ritchie that she appreciated learning from these women and felt it was an honor to be involved in this grant with primarily Yup'ik teachers.

Conclusion and Implications

The experience of participating in a community of learners through this intensive summer course yielded important and significant understanding for us as university instructors and for the teachers serving in the Yup'ik region. Creating a course with the goal of developing a community of learners who worked together to act critically against the dominance of standardized assessments raised challenges and uncovered emotion and pain. Nevertheless, by opening up opportunities for the teachers to draw on their power of place through Indigenous knowledge systems, many practical and culturally congruent assessments were created for use in K–12 classrooms of primarily Yup'ik children. In addition, we found that coteaching and coconstructing this course with both a Yup'ik and non-Yup'ik faculty member provided teachers with valuable models for negotiating course content and class feedback.

This CTAR project left several questions that require further investigation and analysis. First, we would like to explore how the teachers' plans to use Indigenized assessment were implemented once they returned to their school contexts. We would like to investigate the following: Has their practice of assessing students changed? If so, how and in what ways? What were their challenges in implementing the newly developed assessments? Did they face resistance from parents, other teachers, and the administration? How did they manage resistance? Finally, how did the students react to the assessments the teachers developed? What were their successes? By following up with the practicing teachers, we can better understand what kinds of support systems are needed. In addition, we can investigate how this community of learners, developed within the course and through other grant activities, can continue in useful ways.

Finally, we would like to further explore our own practice as teacher educators. We want to continue to reflect on our own practice. We raise such questions as how can we as teacher educators refine and model future courses to enhance the funds of knowledge Indigenous teachers bring to these courses? How can our negotiations as coinstructors be improved to use the strengths we each brought to the course? How can we continue to support teachers in their efforts to develop and implement Indigenous assessments as well as confront assimilationist assessment practices in their teaching contexts? Through these questions, we hope to continue affirming Indigenous knowledge systems through funds of knowledge and supported by local communities of practice.

Notes

The majority of this chapter was published as "Indigenizing Assessment Using Community Funds of Knowledge: A Critical Action Research Study," *Journal of American Indian Education* 20 (3) (2011), and is used with permission from the publisher.

1. Summer is intense for Yup'ik people because it is the short time during which salmon are caught, prepared, and stored. In most cases, these teachers would be at their fish camps with their families and extended families preparing for the winter. Inevitably, being in fish camp was a common part of discussion throughout the summer session.

CHAPTER SIX

Ellangluni

Power, Awareness, and Agency in Language Planning

Patrick E. Marlow and April G. L. Counceller

This chapter focuses on data generated in a summer intensive course investigating language policy and planning as it relates to endangered language contexts. For us, language policy and planning includes both formal governmental (top-down) and community–school–family (bottom-up) efforts to influence the choice and function of linguistic codes (Baldauf 2005, 2006; Cooper 1989). Language policy and planning is a mechanism of both domination by (Tollefson 1991) and a means of resistance to (Lomawaima & McCarty 2002) majority community conceptions of what it means to be a linguistic minority. It is both a political tool (Patrick 2007) and a deeply personal and highly emotional topic of investigation (Hinton & Hale 2001).

The class of six Yup'ik Eskimo and one non-Native master's students (from here on referred to as teachers) was cotaught by a faculty adviser (Patrick E. Marlow) and an Alaska Native (Alutiiq) doctoral student (April G. L. Counceller). The intended outcome for the course was a partial literature review relating to the teachers' own master's thesis work. At the same time, we hoped the course would not only foster an awareness among the teachers of the role language policy has played in the historical (and continuing) oppression of Alaska Native communities (Duchene & Heller 2007; Lomowaima & McCarty 2002; Tollefson 1991) but also empower them to see themselves as change agents in addressing local language goals (Herr & Anderson 2005; Kipp 2000; Patrick 2007).

We begin this chapter with a brief overview of our research methodology, data analysis techniques, theoretical framing, and participants and setting. We then briefly discuss our course planning before moving on to discuss the three primary themes that emerged from our data: power, *ellangluni* (becoming aware), and agency.

Methodology

Following April G. L. Counceller (2010), we describe our methdological framework as Indigenous action research. Indigenous action research integrates core principles of action research (Herr & Anderson 2005; Kemmis & McTaggart 2000), and TribalCrit (Brayboy 2005), an Indigenous research orientation based on critical theory (Foley & Valenzuela 2000; Grand 2000) and influenced by Indigenous research ethics (Smith 1999).

Action research is reflexive, collaborative, and oriented toward positive change (Herr & Anderson 2005). The action research process is not linear but involves a "spiral" of research (plan, act, observe, and reflect), which recasts research as an ongoing process that builds on itself for improvement of both process and project outcome (Herr & Anderson 2005, p. 5).

Like critical theory, TribalCrit seeks to reveal issues of power, ideology, and hegemony in an effort to foster social justice and equality. An outgrowth of critical race theory (Delgado & Stefancic 2001), TribalCrit specifically addresses Native American positions as racialized beings and political entities, as well as colonized peoples (Brayboy 2005). TribalCrit argues that colonialism is "endemic in society" and that countering colonialism requires us to acknowledge Native American epistemologies and support tribal goals of self-determination, sovereignty, and self-identification (Brayboy 2005, p. 430; Writer 2008).

As an Indigenous action research project, the course was designed to bring about positive change within the research community, in this case a class of six Yup'ik Eskimo and one non-Native teacher engaged in language teaching and program development in southwestern Alaska. The course explicitly sought to highlight how language policy has been used as a tool of oppression of Alaska Native communities, as well as how an awareness of such policy can be used to empower participants as change agents in addressing local language goals set by the communities themselves. Course design was cyclical as we responded to and adjusted for participant needs and demands throughout course implementation. Data consist of field notes, class artifacts, and instructors' planning and debriefing sessions, as well as teacher comprehensive exams and final theses.

Data Analysis

Earlier versions of this chapter were presented to the American Anthropological Association and the American Association for Applied Linguistics. In preparation for those presentations, the authors held multiple debriefing sessions to discuss the theoretical framework (Marlow & Counceller 2008) and apply that framework to the data sources already mentioned (Marlow & Counceller 2009). These discussion sessions were recorded, and key sections were transcribed for further analysis. In addition, each author composed a brief history of his or her involvement in both the class and the field of language policy and planning. These brief histories further informed our emerging theoretical framework.

Analysis of the data was cyclical and began with the debriefing sessions. Project artifacts were reviewed independently by each author before and after, as well as jointly during debriefing sessions. Using a constructivist grounded theory approach (Charmaz 2000), the authors coded the data and began organizing the codes into key themes and subthemes. Themes and subthemes were then compared and discussed in light of our emerging theoretical framework, resulting in three primary themes: power, *ellangluni*, and agency.

For us, *power* refers to one's ability to influence the social world through action. *Ellangluni* is a Yup'ik concept that Anna Angiak-Bond (2010, p. 2) defines as "gaining an enlightened understanding of why and how things are or are not." In Yup'ik culture, as in many Indigenous cultures, with awareness comes a moral obligation to act. *Agency* refers to one's ability to act: to use power for the direct benefit of others. Thus, all three concepts are interrelated. Agency requires the power to act, whereas awareness requires that one does act.

Theoretical Framing

Language planning may be defined as the deliberate attempt to influence the acquisition, structure, or function of a language (Cooper 1989; Haugen 1959; Wright 2004). In the endangered language context, language planning generally involves the deliberate attempt to foster language maintenance or revitalization (Fishman 1991; Hinton & Hale 2001; Paulston 1994).

Whereas language policy and planning began as top-down, government-driven strategies to address practical communicative problems within the modern nation state (see Calvet 1998; Fishman 1974; Haugen 1959), by the early 1990s researchers were recognizing that any attempt to influence a minority language situation must have the support of the local community (see Fishman 1991; Kaplan & Baldauf 1997). Around the same time, Indigenous and minority communities faced with language shift started looking to language planning for support to address local language concerns. In the context of widespread language endangerment, in the limelight since the late 1990s (see Abley 2003; Crystal 2000; Nettle & Romaine 2000), much language planning research has addressed the question of *why* preserve endangered languages, as well as *how* (see Fishman 2001; Grenoble & Whaley 1998).

To affect local practice, most scholars agree that language planning efforts in endangered language contexts must *be initiated and controlled* by the community itself (see Hinton & Hale 2001; Fishman 1991; Kaplan & Baldauf 1997). Thus, for both goal setting and policy implementation, the focus has shifted to grassroots, bottom-up language planning, where the agency of communities and the individual is increasingly emphasized (see Hinton & Hale 2001; Ignace 1999). Such approaches prioritize contextualized goal setting and efforts at the micro level (see Baldauf 2005; Burnaby & Reyhner 2002; Sims 2006, Tollefson 2002). In brief, these approaches reflect efforts by local groups (Indigenous people, linguistic minorities, etc.) to determine and shape language situations based on their own needs and priorities, in the contexts that most matter to them.

For us, Indigenous language planning, whether it happens in the school, the home, or the "family–community nexus" (Fishman 1991), is ultimately an exercise in self-determination. K. Tsianina Lomawaima and Teresa L. McCarty (2002) relate self-determination to the American Indian struggle for sovereignty. For them, sovereignty is "the right of a people to self-government, self-determination and self-education. Sovereignty includes the right to linguistic and cultural expression according to local languages and norms" (p. 284). Christina Paulston (1994) makes a much stronger and more controversial claim. For her, language maintenance and revitalization require nationalism or a desire for independent political status and institutions on an independent territory. For Paulston, nationalism provides the necessary "socially mobilizing force" to counter the opportunity and incentives that would otherwise lead to language shift (p. 25–40). Although Joshua A. Fishman (1991) avoids the terms *nationalism*, *sovereignty*, and *self-determination* in his seminal volume *Reversing Language Shift* and prefers the less polarizing phrases "local options" and "local control," his well-known Graded Intergenerational Disruption Scale,[1] ending as it does in the local language being used in higher government and educational spheres, certainly implies similar concepts.

Whether framed as sovereignty, nationalism, or local control, Indigenous language planning is frequently a part of larger efforts to gain recognition as a (semi)autonomous group (Paulston 1994), as well as gain control over ancestral lands and the institutions (e.g., school, local government) of modern life (Fishman 1991; Patrick 2007; Stairs 1994). To be successful, therefore, Indigenous language planning must support the community to identify and achieve its language goals as well as the social, political, and/or economic goals relating to language revitalization and maintenance.

Participants and Setting

The class was organized and taught by a faculty member, Patrick E. Marlow, and an Alaska Native (Alutiiq) PhD candidate, April G. L. Counceller. Students (the teachers) in the class included five Yup'ik and one non-Native masters's degree candidates (for a more detailed discussion see Chapter 1). Although two of the teachers had taken the course two years before (and both earned high grades), they were advised to retake the course for two reasons. First, course content had changed significantly. Second, the course assignments became part of the literature review required for their theses.

Course Planning

Course development was a collaborative process between Marlow and Counceller. The course was based on one that Marlow taught frequently (seven times between 2002 and 2008) as a stacked (undergraduate/graduate) course for a general audience. Counceller's experience in teaching at the college level was an introductory course on the Alutiiq language. She approached the experience of coteaching the course more from the perspective of a student, as she was at a similar stage in her doctoral studies as the teachers were in their master's coursework. She came to the class from a position as an academic outsider, having gained practical knowledge of language policy and planning from six years working in a language revitalization program in her home community. She was also aware that as an Alaska Native PhD student, she stood as an example for the master's students (teachers), although this was complicated by the fact that she was from a different language community (Alutiiq as opposed to Yup'ik) and the teachers were older than she was, some with more practical experience in language planning.

Content was intended to cover a variety of topics, including official policies in the United States and Alaska (see Crawford 2004; Marlow 2004), the status of Indigenous languages generally, and an understanding of why and how communities shift languages (see Fishman 1991; Paulston 1994; Woodbury 1993, 1998; Wyman 2012). For this offering, we strengthened content on formal policy as it relates to language policy and Alaska Native and American Indian (AN/AI) students in the K–12 school system as well as added content on globalization (Duchene & Heller 2007; Wright 2004), grassroots language planning (Gegeo & Watson-Gegeo 1999), and action research (Herr & Anderson 2005). Strengthening the course in this way was a deliberate attempt to foster political consciousness. As many authors have noted, language policy in the United States is largely a subset of educational policy (Crawford 2004); in the case of AN/AI communities, this policy history is also a story of historical (and continuing) oppression (Lomowaima & McCarty 2002; Tollefson 1991). In the context of this history, we wanted the teachers to discover for themselves what the laws actually say and how those laws are and have been interpreted at the federal, state, and local levels. We also wanted the teachers to have an understanding of how global forces can affect life in even the remotest of Alaska villages. Toward this end, we encouraged discussion of the risks and opportunities for threatened languages presented by globalization (McCarty 2003; Wright 2004).

The focus of grassroots language planning on collaborative ownership of research agendas, as well as its focus on positive change and community responsibility and reciprocity, derived directly from Counceller's experience as a community language activist engaged in Indigenous action research. Counceller has worked in language revitalization and education in Kodiak, Alaska, since 2002, managing a series of grant-funded projects for the Native-run Alutiiq Museum and Archaeological Repository. As other Kodiak regions have begun language revitalization projects in recent years, community organizations like the museum and their partners have worked hard to maintain collaborative relationships and keep efforts aligned with local needs. Communication and partnerships have been fostered by a grassroots regional language advisory committee, allowing the responsibility for language revitalization to spread throughout Alutiiq tribal and educational entities rather than being controlled by one institution.

Discussion of Themes

Power

As noted earlier, the course was intended to foster a political consciousness among the teachers. By this we mean not only an understanding of the political nature of language policy and planning but also an appreciation of their own power to act in response to, support of, and creation of language policies and plans that support (or mitigate) their personal and communal language goals. Key concepts that were difficult but important to the thinking of several of the teachers (and thus became central to ongoing class discussion) included ideology, hegemony, power, choice, and manufacture of consent (as discussed by Tollefson 1991).

In our efforts to help them gain control over new (and often difficult) vocabulary, the teachers were asked to identify key words from their daily readings, which they would define in small groups and place on posters around the room. This was a difficult task for some, with different groups occasionally coming up with very different definitions for the same word. For example, the following definitions of *ideology* and *hegemony* were all posted on the wall on the same day.

Ideology:

- The normal unconscious assumptions that many see as common sense, often dependent upon those who are in power in society
- An assumption/ideas/values/beliefs toward an economic and political philosophy or program

Hegemony:

- The successful production of ideology
- Then a dominating group influences production/reproduction of ideology
- Control by one group over society (usually political)

Rather than being seen as problematic, variations in definitions were taken as opportunities for the teachers to share their understandings of the concepts and discuss those understandings in relation to their sociopolitical contexts and emerging thesis research.

The concepts of power, ideology, and choice were particularly difficult for some teachers to grasp. For James W. Tollefson (1991), *ideology* refers to unconscious assumptions that come to be seen as common sense. *Hege-*

mony, in turn, is the successful reproduction of ideology. Both are related to power insofar as assumptions that come to be seen as common sense depend on the ability of those with more power in society to gain the consent (manufacture of consent) of subordinate groups. Within this framework, choice is never truly free, but always proscribed by power and ideology. In other words, those with more power have greater freedom of choice (i.e., more predefined alternatives to choose from) than those with less power. This power structure is maintained through the reproduction of ideology (hegemony) and the manufacture of consent (Tollefson 1991, p. 10–16).

Prior to class discussion, the teachers generally accepted the idea that individual (and by extension community) choice is "free" and that commonsense ideas like *English is necessary to get a job* are nothing more than common sense. As they struggled to unpack the concepts of power, choice, and ideology, however, they began to see their own actions and personal as well as communal histories in a new light. Turning first to the idea of choice, teacher 1 considers the possibility that the community's power to choose is illusory and past choices are simply the result of a history of domination by more powerful outsiders.[2] Teacher 2 considers the effect of school policy in constraining her ability to choose to speak Yugtun to her child at home. Teacher 3 considers how economic pressures constrain choice in language of instruction.

> The *Webster's Dictionary* has defined choice as: "power of choosing." Today, the people in [village] have a choice of sending our children to boarding schools to get "better education." We also have an option for our children to learn through Yup'ik or English. But what does it mean to have a choice? Am I really being given a choice? That is the question I have begun to ask myself since taking this class. Have we been spoon-fed the idea that because we are "free" to choose, we are in control and we have the power? In the Western world, having choices is synonymous with having power. Many times the Yup'ik people are unconsciously aware that the choices we are given and make are a result of our histories. This paper will look at choice in the context [of] school and it will look specifically [at] Indigenous peoples' choice when it comes to school. (teacher 1, midterm exam)

> I want to understand exactly what the structures are in the school that affect the decisions of language planning. . . . Do their policies

> play a role in my decision to speak in my first language to my child or not? This has allowed me to realize that the bigger world does have an effect on my decisions. (teacher 2, literature review)

> Many people from the region are also moving to Anchorage and the larger cities for jobs and economic reasons due to the high costs of living here in rural Alaska. What is going to happen to their choice of Yup'ik and language in the schools? (teacher 3, comprehensive exam)

Turning to ideology, teacher 2 questions the assumption that outsiders are inherently better qualified for high-paying teaching jobs, and teacher 4 links ideologies supporting the dominance of English to recent changes in language of instruction in some communities:

> In the school setting, the majority of high-paying positions are held by certified teachers who are not from the village and are Kassaqs [white people]. So the history of education in the community stems from those coming [from] outside to hold these jobs is an "accepted norm" (ideology). To be able to teach English, one must be very good at using English. (teacher 2, comprehensive exam)

> The ideology in this region has been that in order to succeed in life, you have to know the English language. Even though there is the thought that our schools in the [local school district] have a choice of whether or not to use Yugtun in the lower grades (kindergarten to third grade), some schools have chosen to switch from Yugtun to English because of the fear of not passing the High School Graduation Qualifying Exam (HSGQE). (teacher 4, comprehensive exam)

This exploration of power, choice, and ideology led several teachers to rethink or redirect their thesis research. One teacher, Jill Hoffman, who wanted to look at the reasons parents enrolled their students in immersion or English school, realized it was not as simple as looking at a parent's perception of risks and benefits, but what social forces constrained or enhanced that parent's choices. She wondered aloud in class if the parents really had any choice at all. In the poster in Figure 6.1, Hoffman rephrases this question in the title "English or Yup'ik School: A parental choice?" She then relates this question to three separate themes she planned to take up in the literature review for her thesis. In the middle of the poster, following Tollefson (1991), Hoffman defines *choice* as inherently limited

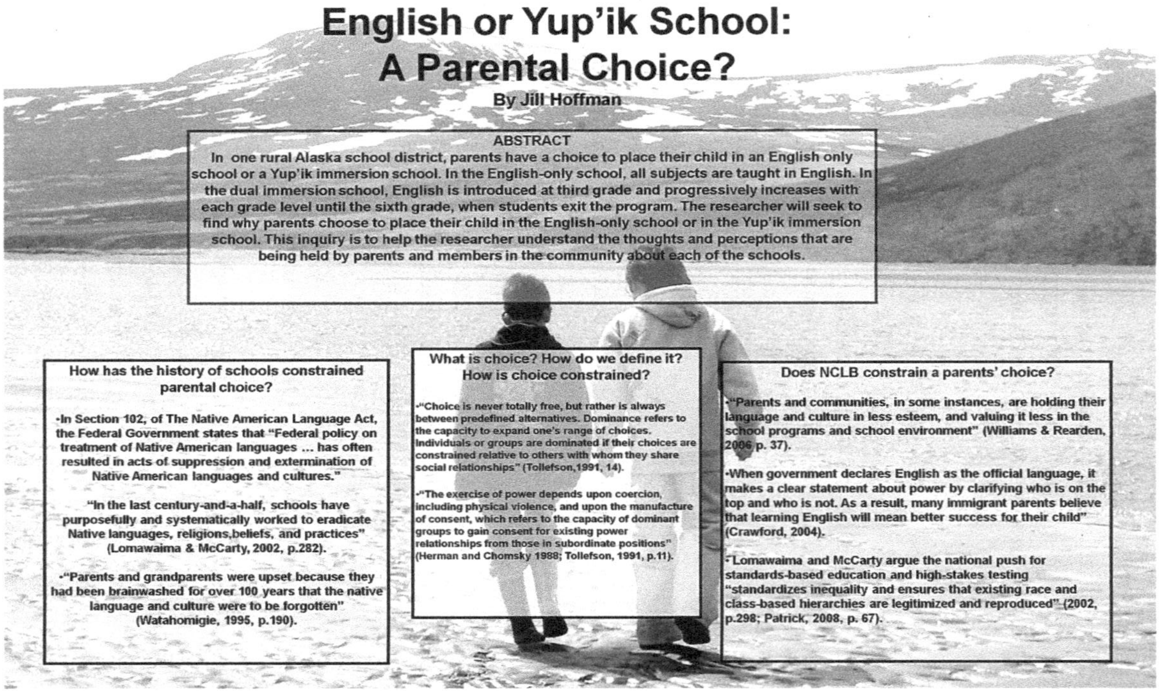

Figure 6.1. SLATE literature review poster (source: Jill Hoffman, summer 2008)

and related to the level of power and autonomy enjoyed by the person making the choice. On the left side of the poster, she investigates the role of schools and schooling in limiting choice and coercing American Indian and Alaska Native communities to assimilate into whitestream culture. On the right side of the poster, she extends this history of coercion to the No Child Left Behind legislation.

Another teacher, Renee Green, was conducting research into the role of schools in language revitalization. She came to understand that this relationship is more complicated than she originally thought. Rather than being a straightforward "choice" freely made by the community, language choice in schooling ultimately requires Yup'ik people to be agents in their own struggle to resist the majority community's power to limit choices and thereby mold and control Alaska Native people (see Figure 6.2).

Becoming Aware

Throughout the course, the teachers approached questions of language shift and revitalization from a highly personal, very local perspective. All seven women were teachers, six were mothers, five were Yugtun speakers. Not surprisingly, therefore, many approached the course simultaneously from their personal positions as parents attempting to raise Yup'ik children and as educators trying to understand the role the school and they themselves play in language maintenance and shift.

In class discussions the key word *ellangluni* (becoming aware) recurred frequently. As Angiak-Bond (2010, p. 2) explains: "Becoming aware, *ellangluni*, can be defined as gaining an enlightened understanding of why and how things are or are not. To become aware is to have an 'ah-ha!' moment to make a connection and see things in a new way. These moments allow individuals to make positive changes in their lives to become better people."

As a group and as individuals, the class struggled to become aware of their personal place in Yup'ik shift and revitalization. Key questions asked by teachers in individual theses included, but were not limited to, the following:

- What led to language shift in the first place?
- How did their actions as parents and teachers, and those of their parents and families, play into that shift?
- What could they do personally to foster language maintenance and revitalization for the next generation?

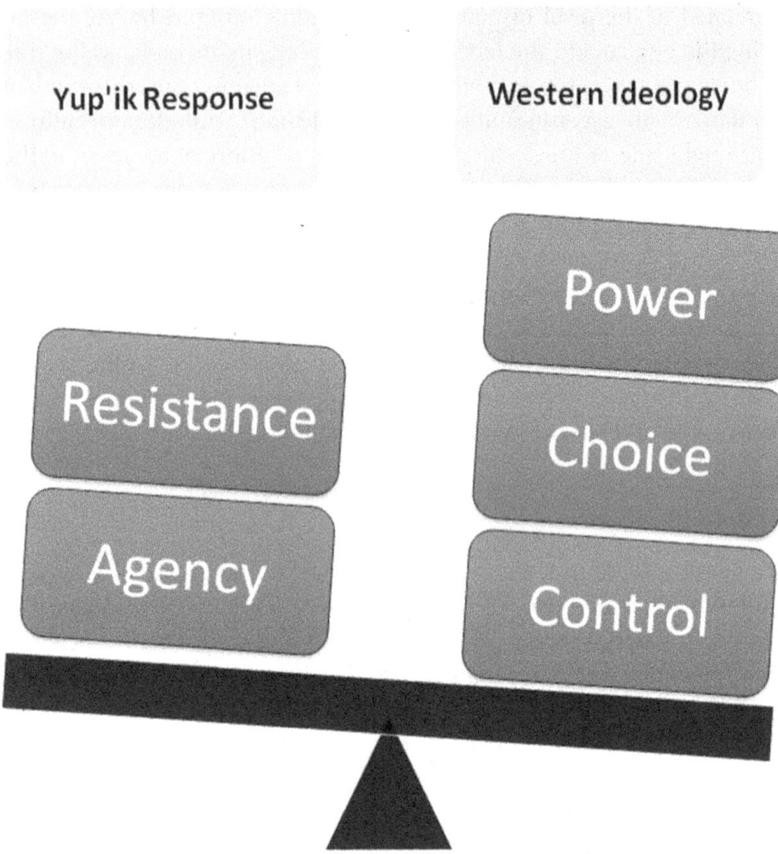

Figure 6.2. Diagram from SLATE literature review poster (source: Renee Green, summer 2008)

Of course, each of the teachers developed and addressed their own research questions, and each emphasized issues and questions they felt were most relevant to their own situation. However, when we look at the work of the class as a whole, we find that the above questions are addressed repeatedly and from different perspectives.

In Yugtun, *ellangluni* is not a passive concept. As the following quotes taken from teacher theses demonstrate, awareness links back to the individual's responsibility to act for positive change within the community.

> I couldn't believe how naive I was about maintaining my first language. From my experience, simply becoming aware of the situation is the key to revitalizing Yup'ik, to finding the desire, and the purpose to

> keep it going. The next step is to involve the community somehow, to help them become aware like I did. (Angiak-Bond 2010, p. 53)

> We understand our own level of awareness and need to make sure that we guide others toward that understanding. (Michael 2010, p. 23)

> We feel the responsibility to spread awareness, which becomes both a burden and a thrilling task to undertake. In all that we see, hear and feel, we see possibilities of change. (Michael 2010, p. 58)

> This is exactly what needs to happen. Once awareness is spread among our people, we *can* work together as a community to get our language back. It all begins with us. If we support one another and take the pride of being *Yup'ik* . . . we can begin the process of beginning to speak our heritage languages. (Amos-Andrew 2010, p. 24)

As the quotes demonstrate, *ellangluni* implies not only an awareness of the facts but also the responsibility to act on that awareness and the power to do so. In other words, a deeper understanding comes with the responsibility to share that understanding with others and to advocate and work for the survival and betterment of the community as a whole. This belief is shared by many Indigenous societies around the world, as Counceller, writing about Indigenous epistemology as it is expressed among the Alutiiq of Kodiak Island, explains:

> This sense of responsibility in knowledge . . . requires knowledge gained through research to be relevant to community needs and . . . is related to a concern in Indigenous communities for community survival (Brayboy & Maughan 2009). In the past, this survival was in terms of physical survival, health and well-being. Today, survival has shifted meaning, at least in part, to mean resistance against assimilation in order to perpetuate community and cultural survival. This perspective on survival has been called survivance by Vizenor (1994a), and refers to the strategies used by communities to resist, adapt and accommodate in order to survive in difficult times (Powell 2002; Vizenor 1994b, 2009). (2010, p. 78–79)

Agency

As the class evolved, literature on grassroots language planning (Gegeo & Watson-Gegeo 1999; Kipp 2000; McCarty 2003) and action research

(Herr & Anderson 2005) allowed the teachers to deepen their awareness (*ellangluni*), further develop a sense of their own power, and ultimately seize on their own agency to bring about local change.

This shift in agency can be seen in the teachers' growing willingness to advocate on behalf of their communities. One example of this growing agency occurred on July 18, 2008. The class as a whole was engaged in an unstructured discussion regarding their individual roles in fostering language and culture maintenance and countering hegemonic school practices that they felt continued to marginalize some children and some communities. One teacher, a Yup'ik woman in her mid-thirties, was openly struggling with the idea of agency. Although she felt deeply that she needed to be a voice for both children and elders, she did not believe she was old enough or experienced enough to be taken seriously as an advocate. She turned to two other Yup'ik women, each ten to fifteen years older than she, and explicitly invited them to tell her how they managed to move into such roles within their communities. One woman told a story of how she was taught to lead by example. She explained how when she first returned to her home village as a teacher, people acted differently around her; some even avoided her. Afraid she might further alienate herself from the community, she sought advice from her father. He told her that she should not seek to give advice or comment on things other people were doing. If she were patient and willing to demonstrate her knowledge and professionalism as a teacher without comment, people would begin to see what she had to offer and they would seek her advice (which they ultimately did).

Today both the teacher who sought the advice and her colleague who provided it are leading advocates for Yugtun programming in their school district. Both now work in the Curriculum and Instruction department, where they are responsible for leading the implementation of a new K–6 Yugtun-English dual language program intended to replace the early transition K–3 Yugtun programs in place in the region since the early 1970s (see Marlow et al. 2011). As Marlow explained in a faculty debriefing session, this is just one example of how these teachers are acting on their new found awareness: "The big step for me is ultimately these teachers become themselves the leaders . . . that they are pushing it forward themselves in some format. Which is why I am so thrilled . . . that [Name] is at the district office and I am so thrilled that [Name] is talking about going on and getting her principal's license, and [Name], after resisting it for so long, is now saying, 'I should be involved in planning for my school and helping to decide what kind of language program we should have.' So all of those things are part of moving forward. . . To use their phrase, they are becoming aware."

Conclusions and Implications

As noted in the introduction to this chapter, the course sought to "empower the teachers to see themselves as change agents." Some readers may reject the term *empower* here on the grounds that it is paternalistic and therefore works to disempower the very people we seek to empower. We agree. In virtually all dictionary definitions of *empower.* those providing the empowerment are the agents of the action. They (or we the instructors, in this case) are invested with the ability and/or authority to grant power or enable or encourage the teachers to seize power. The teachers themselves remain passive recipients of this empowerment.

However, through the Yup'ik concept of *ellangluni*, the course was moved beyond this paternalistic model of empowerment. As noted, *ellangluni* is not a passive concept. Unlike "empowerment," *ellangluni* cannot be given, granted, or taught. It must come from within the individual and, once arrived at, it requires action. This active relationship between awareness and action in many ways mirrors Paolo Freire's (2000) concept of praxis (discussed in the introduction to this book), through which teaching and learning reflect a transformative process that can help us challenge and reflect on our long-held assumptions about the status quo. Like praxis, *ellangluni* is an active, transformative process that can help us question our theories about and practices in the world and act on them. Although it is reminiscent of praxis, however, we maintain that *ellangluni* is a unique Indigenous concept deriving from a local epistemology emphasizing individual responsibility and communal reciprocity in action (Counceller 2010).

It is important to note that as an Indigenous Yup'ik (and Alutiiq) concept, *ellangluni* was not a planned part of the course syllabus. It entered the class spontaneously through the teachers themselves and became a way for them (and us) to understand the material and their/our relationship to it. In this way, *ellangluni* became the organizing principle for understanding the personal and communal transformation that occurred within the course and the Second Language Acquisition Teacher Education (SLATE) program as a whole.

In many ways, the course content was already known to the teachers. As noted in the "Participants and Setting" section, two of the teachers had taken a version of the course two years before. More than this, however, all the teachers knew that the educational system had oppressed them. They knew that earlier (and current) policy had repressed the language and encouraged shift of language, culture, and identity. As teachers they were well aware of their personal role within the institution of schooling to act (or not) for change. Yet this knowledge of the facts did not reach the level of awareness implied by *ellangluni*. In many ways, this awareness was like Counceller's initial awareness of her father's actions to repair a fishnet:

> For me, becoming aware [*llangluni* in Alutiiq], comes in more than one stage. The first stage is the point at which your earliest memories begin. That is when, as I have been told, you "come to" and begin your life as an aware person. In my mind, though, there is another stage, when adult learning and awareness begin to take hold. I have many memories of early childhood, but most of them are vague—I wasn't fully present in the moment, and not fully absorbing what I was being taught. I recall many times when I would help my dad, holding the corkline of the gillnet as he stitched on the webbing or repaired holes. But instead of learning how to do what he was doing, I'd be looking at the clouds. Or sometimes I'd watch but not be following what he was doing. We moved to Kodiak before I reached adolescence, and I just never learned those skills as I would have if I had been helping him with the net as I grew older. And now I couldn't repair or construct a net to save my life. I was not at that second stage of awareness when we lived in the village, and I still feel a sense of loss today, that I never learned those skills. I can tell you that if my dad was working on the net today that I would be right there paying attention. And then I would make my own. (debriefing session)

As Counceller explains, she participated in the activity; she was aware of the activity; yet she was not fully present to the activity. It was not until later, when she was ready, that she became fully aware of the importance of her participation and felt the need to participate actively. This then is what the course and the SLATE program helped accomplish—they provided a framework for deepening an awareness that was in many ways already present. In contrast to Counceller, however, we hope this awareness has not come too late.

We do not claim here that the course fostered *ellangluni* on its own. Such a claim would reduce *ellangluni* to an Indigenous form of empowerment. Agency would remain with the instructors and the syllabus, and the teachers would be reduced to passive recipients of this empowerment. Thus, although we do feel the course worked as a catalyst to focus the teachers' attention on specific issues, we freely acknowledge that the teachers' personal histories, their own research, and other coursework (see especially Chapter 5) all conspired to prepare them for this new level of awareness. However, once explicitly aware, as Counceller and the teachers themselves tell us, they were responsible for using their personal and institutional power to act (agency). In this way, the teachers themselves are continuing the cycle of Indigenous action research that began in this course, continued with their own theses, and continues today in their roles as teachers, school administrators, parents, and community members (see Chapter 7) as they continue to share and expand their own awareness and influence language and culture maintenance and foster social justice throughout the Yup'ik region.

Notes

1. Similar to the Richter scale, Fishman's (1991) Graded Intergenerational Disruption Scale (GIDS) may be understood from high (stage 8: most disrupted) to low (stage 1: least disrupted). Stage 8: Most remaining users of Xish (the endangered language) are socially isolated old folks, and Xish needs to be reassembled from their mouths and memories and taught to demographically unconcentrated adults. Stage 7: Most users of Xish are a socially integrated and ethnolinguistically active population, but they are beyond childbearing age. Stage 6: The attainment of intergenerational informal oralcy and its demographic concentration and institutional reinforcement. Stage 5: Xish literacy in home, school, and community, but without taking on extra-communal reinforcement of such literacy. Stage 4: Xish in lower education that meets the requirements of compulsory education laws. Stage 3: Use of Xish in the lower work sphere (outside of the Xish neighborhood/community) involving interaction between Xmen (endangered language community members) and Ymen (majority community members). Stage 2: Xish in lower governmental services and mass media but not in the higher spheres of either. Stage 1: Some use of Xish in higher level educational, occupational, governmental, and media efforts (but without the additional safety provided by political independence).

2. Student work is cited in two ways throughout the chapter. Published works (e.g., theses, articles, posters) are cited by author and year. When the work is unpublished (e.g., class notes, exams), the author is identified by number (e.g., teacher 1, teacher 2).

CHAPTER SEVEN

Conversations

Patrick E. Marlow, Marilee Coles-Ritchie,
Sabine Siekmann, and Joan Parker Webster

This final chapter derives from a three-day summative program evaluation session with the Second Language Acquisition Teacher Education (SLATE) faculty. This evaluation session was conducted in November 2010, six months after the majority of the program participants (seventeen of the eighteen teachers and one of the four PhD candidates) had successfully completed their degree programs. Prior to the evaluation session, the eighteenth and final teacher completed her degree (August 2010) and two additional doctoral candidates successfully defended their theses; the fourth PhD candidate was involved in data analysis. Thus, with the project largely complete, the faculty met to discuss the successes and challenges of the program as well as reflect on what might have been done differently and what the next steps might be.

Methodology

The entire three-day session included both evaluation and analysis. The evaluation session consisted of five 90–120-minute discussion periods. All discussion periods were recorded, resulting in approximately eight hours of audio files and thirty pages of typed field notes. Although discussions often continued during breaks, no notes were taken and important points were returned to when the session resumed. Although the faculty did not prepare formal questions and no one person was designated the interviewer for the purposes of the sessions, key questions were tacitly agreed on (e.g., What constitutes program success? What challenges come to mind for you as you reflect back on the program?), and faculty took turns questioning and encouraging one another to speak. Field notes were taken in turn by each of the faculty members. While taking field notes, faculty tended to adopt the observer role, rejoining the conversation only when they felt particularly compelled to do so.

Data Analysis

The faculty met on day 3 to review and analyze the compiled field notes. Using a constructivist grounded theory approach (Charmaz 2000), faculty coded the data and began organizing the codes into themes and subthemes. Three primary themes emerged: (1) building a community of learners through research, (2) transforming pedagogy, and (3) defining success.

We used initial theme outlines to guide transcription of key sections of the evaluation session. We engaged in a process similar to reconstructive analysis (Carsprecken 1996) in which sections of dialogue were edited, reordered, and occasionally expanded on to create compact and coherent discussions of each of the three major themes. To maintain the integrity of the original conversation, frequent member checks were conducted. This process of data manipulation and review, in keeping with a constructivist grounded theory (Charmaz 2000), provided multiple opportunities for all conversational participants to view the original data and expand on our initial understandings of that data. As a result, new ideas developed and new questions emerged, resulting in recoding of the data multiple times.

This process resulted in the refinement of three major themes with twelve subthemes and five recurrent themes. Major themes are seen as primary topics of conversation, and subthemes are seen as subtopics. In contrast, recurrent themes are repeated throughout the dialogue and form linkages between the topics of conversation (major and subthemes). In this chapter we discuss two major themes along with the seven relevant subthemes and three recurrent themes listed in Tables 7.1 and 7.2.

Discussion of Themes: Major and Subthemes

Building a Community of Learners through Research

The Graduate Research Collaboratives (GRCs) were the central design element unique to the SLATE project. Through the GRCs, faculty sought

Table 7.1. Major Themes and Subthemes

Themes	*Subthemes*	*Description*
Building a research community	Choice of research community	"Assignment to" vs. "choice of" GRC affected the development of the research community
	Peer support	Building social connections between the teachers as peers
	Faculty as outsider	The faculty members' positioning as white academics and outsiders affected the development of the research community
	PhD candidate as mediator	The PhD candidates' positioning as Alaska Natives helped bridge between the faculty/academy and the teachers
Defining success	Program completion	Success is defined as the teachers completing the program
	Institutionalization	Success is defined as institutionalization of the program both within the academy/university and the region
	Capacity building	Success is defined as laying the groundwork for the teachers to take the lead themselves

to foster research collaborations between and among all members of each of the four GRCs (Pedagogy, Multiliteracies, Assessment, and Language Policy and Planning). As noted many times before, each GRC was headed by a faculty member, and each consisted of one Alaska Native PhD candidate and up to six master's candidates. GRC meetings were intended to facilitate the development of individual and group research agendas, as well as allow for continued exchange among peers, doctoral students, and faculty members.

The GRC design for research reflects the influence of sociocultural

Table 7.2. Recurrent Themes

Recurrent Theme	*Description*
Time	Time pressure felt by the teachers or faculty due to either the intensive nature of the project or outside demands on an individual's time
Trust	Building trust between the teachers and the faculty
Leadership	Encouraging the teachers and PhD candidates to take on leadership roles, either now or in the future

theory on the theoretical orientation of the SLATE faculty. As we wrote the grant narrative, we envisioned creating communities of researchers and learners based on Lev Vygotsky's idea (1978) that human learning and development are complexly woven in social interaction. For us, both learning and research are collaborative activities, and as such both engage novices and experts in jointly constructed activity (Rogoff 1993). In the GRCs, the faculty members, PhD candidates, and teachers were all novices in different ways and at different times. The faculty members were learning how to mentor Yup'ik teachers, the PhD candidates were learning how to mediate between the faculty members and teachers, and the teachers were learning how to engage in the research process. All members of the GRCs provided mentorship, gave explanations, and offered support at various junctures and for important purposes during the research process. Within this process, there were a number of success stories as well as tensions. For us as faculty, these successes and tensions fell into four major subthemes: choice of research community, peer support, faculty as outsider, and PhD candidate as mediator.

CHOICE OF RESEARCH COMMUNITY. For the GRCs to reach their potential, it was necessary for teachers to select (or be assigned to) a GRC from the very beginning of the program. However, as the following faculty exchange shows, choice was limited by the nature of the program. Teachers were able to select from one of four topic areas, but this choice occurred largely before the teachers had an opportunity to take classes or get to know the faculty or their peers. Furthermore, grant time constraints (i.e., the push to finish theses and degrees within the grant period) put additional pressure on faculty to expediently assign teachers to individual GRCs. To balance these needs and pressures, faculty ultimately delayed GRC selection/assignment until the end of the first summer session.

COLES-RITCHIE: But wasn't their choice of GRC somewhat limited? I mean they were able to choose the research area but not the people they would work with. And that meant it took time to develop the relationships, and the trust they needed to really collaborate with their faculty member and with each other.

SIEKMANN: It was a little more complicated than that. I remember we tried to put the teachers in GRCs based on the research interest they gave in their application packets, but it was just too hard to figure out where to put people.

MARLOW: Then there is that idea of "where to put people." That was another reason we decided to wait until after the first summer session was over and they managed to write their initial research proposal. We wanted to give them more time and a bit more autonomy in choosing their GRC.

COLES-RITCHIE: I just can't imagine what it must have been like for them. I mean most of them hadn't even taken a class in their research area yet. The classes in assessment, language policy and planning, and multiliteracies weren't even offered until the second summer.

MARLOW: But we couldn't wait. The time constraints of the grant funding simply did not allow for it.

An additional pressure was the need/desire to balance the work equally among the faculty. In the initial grant narrative, each GRC was imagined to include five students. In reality, however, some research areas were more popular or, as Marilee Coles-Ritchie explains, simply better understood by the teachers. Distribution of teachers across GRCs therefore was uneven, resulting in larger cohorts for Pedagogy and Multiliteracies (five and six, respectively) and smaller cohorts for Assessment and Language Policy and Planning (three and four, respectively).

COLES-RITCHIE: Initially, teachers just don't think of assessment as especially compelling. So when they initially enroll in an assessment course they are not very excited. By the time it ends, they realize how creative they can be with assessment and how closely it relates to instruction. But without that course to kick it off, it is hard to get people excited about doing assessment, which meant there were fewer teachers doing it.

PEER SUPPORT. Once formed, the GRCs provided the social support, including peer-to-peer interaction, necessary for the teachers to develop their own understandings of the academic material and complete the program. As the following discussion shows, breaking the initial cohort of twenty graduate students into four smaller, focused research groups allowed students with a variety of interactive styles to feel comfortable and form the supportive peer relationships needed to complete an intensive program.

MARLOW: When I had dinner with Atan and Rachel just a couple weeks ago, I asked them, "What about SLATE should the university be emulating? What was it that really worked for you guys?"

And they both emphasized the small groups. The cohort model was great. We were this big group, but we didn't remain a big group. We were these smaller groups within the big group, and these smaller groups for them were really key socially and academically, I think, to allow them to get through. And if we had just been one big group, I don't think it would have worked.

COLES-RITCHIE: I think my group's small size really helped us to interact and to share ideas openly. It was also easier for us to find time to meet. One student told me "because we were such a small group [we got] much more personalized support not only from the instructor but also from [each other]."

MARLOW: But even for the teachers who preferred to work alone, I think the social interaction from just being part of a GRC was essential for successful completion of the program. I know in my own graduate experience I really needed that social support. Without it, I would not have finished myself.

SIEKMANN: I agree. [Name] wasn't comfortable negotiating so much with the other teachers and she preferred to work on her own. She was very engaged, but struggled with her writing. But without the GRC I don't think she would have made it.

Although the GRCs were highly structured academic groups with a faculty adviser leading weekly meetings with focused discussion points and specific intended outcomes, they also provided the teachers with a key opportunity to self-organize. As Joan Parker Webster explains, by providing opportunities for both goal-oriented and strategic conversations (organized GRC meetings) as well as opportunities for casual peer-to-peer interaction, the GRC model allowed the teachers to develop deeper understandings of the academic material and how it related to their own research and themselves.

PARKER WEBSTER: I also think the GRCs allowed people to self-organize. When they were together, I think they self-organized. And that is just part of how human systems work. They do self-organize. Habermas (1987) would also say that it is action oriented to understanding. See I think a lot of the GRC conversations were goal oriented and strategic. You come together for a specific purpose and goal. And that is one type of communicative action. But it does not create that deep understanding that is inherent in communicative action toward understanding. Where

> you self-organize and you are working toward multiple perspectives and coming to a shared agreement about something. Which is quite different from goal-oriented or strategic communicative action. And it changes all the time.

FACULTY AS OUTSIDER. Within the SLATE project the faculty were well aware of their positioning as well as their strengths and weaknesses. None of the faculty were community members. To varying degrees, all were outsiders working within an Indigenous context. As such, we claimed differing degrees of experience but no expertise in Alaska Native or Yup'ik ways of knowing and doing things. As Sabine Siekmann explains, given the faculty members' outsidered position, a degree of distrust on the part of the teachers was to be expected: "When we started, there wasn't trust between us. The teachers didn't know us; they didn't know our intentions. They very reasonably assumed our intentions were those of the academic who flies in, takes data, and goes away and publishes and aggrandizes themselves." The most extreme examples of this sort of self-aggrandizement through research on Indigenous peoples are clearly historical, as this example from April G. L. Counceller (Marlow & Counceller 2008), citing Tamara Bray and Thomas Killion (1994) and Gordon Pullar (1994) illustrates:

> In 1930–34 Aleš Hrdlička and an archaeology team from the Smithsonian dug up the remains of nearly a thousand individuals from the community graveyard in Larsen Bay, an Alutiiq (Sugpiaq/Pacific Eskimo) community on Kodiak Island, Alaska (Bray & Killion 1994). My grandfather was about 10 years old at the time. He told me that Dr. Hrdlička would offer village children a dime if they were able to find and bring him a human bone. Villagers at that time did not feel that they had the authority to complain about the "archaeology" project, although reportedly the team unearthed modern graves from the 1918 flu epidemic along with prehistoric ones. (Pullar 1994, p. 21)

Although grave robbing masquerading as archeology may never have been the norm within the academy, Alaska Native communities today often regard researchers of all types with caution or even suspicion. Linguists conducting fieldwork on highly endangered languages may be told that they are in fact stealing the very languages they are attempting to document. Other social science researchers may be denied access to a community because reports by previous researchers were felt to embarrass or belittle the community in some way.

Overcoming this well-founded and firmly rooted distrust was essential for the program's success. Socializing one on one with the teachers was perhaps the most important key to building healthy, trusting faculty-teacher relationships. As the following exchange illustrates, faculty travel to visit individual teachers in their home villages was a turning point. Although such visits required a full day's travel to and from remote villages, beginning in spring 2008 faculty committed themselves to multiple two- and three-day visits with every teacher. These visits allowed faculty and teachers the opportunity to get to know each other as well as focus on individual research and writing assignments.

SIEKMANN: I was trying to figure out when things started to really gel. And I realized a key moment was when we went out to see "our people." Going out to the villages in spring 2008 to work one on one with the students really solidified our relationships. That was a clear signal to them of our commitment, and for me it was a real eye-opener as to what it means, how far away it is, how the world looks different when you are in the village [see Chapter 1]. Putting yourself out there and putting yourself in a situation where you needed them, the teachers, because you were on their turf.

COLES-RITCHIE: There is an element of openness that comes from not just quality but quantity time spent with people. When you are in the village there is down time, there is meeting time, there is just sitting and talking about families, and meeting families that is not attached to the academics. I think just spending down time together helped me to build some trust with my group. We became real people after visiting them on their turf.

MARLOW: It definitely changed the social dynamic. I remember every time I went to visit [Name] in [Village], she would basically grab me by the arm and she would take me around and introduce me, "This is my professor." She would tell everyone. "This is my professor. He's come to work with me." And that also allowed her at some level to turn to other school personnel and say, "Oh no, my professor is here, I have to work on this."

Of course, travel in the Alaska bush is not always predictable. Each visit required two commercial jet airline flights (from Fairbanks to Bethel via

Anchorage) and a flight on a small bush plane (from Bethel to the village). Weather was often an issue. Failure to visit a village could ultimately undermine a faculty–teacher relationship.

> MARLOW: A failure on my part was that I never made it to [Village 1].
> PARKER WEBSTER: And I never made it to [Village 2]. [Name] always felt isolated—and I didn't get out to her village. I felt really bad about that. Going out would have made a big difference to her.
> MARLOW: And in both of those cases, those teachers struggled more than others. And I honestly believe that a significant part of that was the sense that they were isolated and that we perhaps were less interested in working with them for some reason other than the bad weather keeping us from traveling.

Perhaps even more than physical distance, language separated the faculty and the teachers. None of the faculty spoke Yugtun. The language of the institution and by extension the academy was English. In a conscious effort to open the academy to the teachers, faculty accepted initial program applications in either Yugtun or English. Although only one teacher submitted her application in Yugtun, we felt it was an important symbolic act at the beginning of the program. This same teacher later noted in private conversation that accepting her application in Yugtun was an important act of validation for her as a Yup'ik person. This simple act of validation could have been seen as empty symbolism if it had not been for other efforts by the faculty to invite Yugtun into the program. As Siekmann explains, by explicitly inviting Yugtun into the classroom she was able to foster trust, teacher ownership and appropriate peer-to-peer interaction, even when she herself did not speak Yugtun:

> As a language teacher, I thought a lot about the fact that the teachers are Yugtun speakers and I am not, and I want them to use Yugtun but how do I do that? I can't remember when the switch happened, when we switched from English to Yugtun. The process of how we got there was a little fuzzy. Except for [Name 1] they were all teaching Yugtun and [Name 1] was the only one teaching in an English-speaking school. I recognized that they could all speak Yugtun . . . and I would try to foster that. I said, "We aren't having these meetings for me, they are for you." I had [Name 2] and [Name 3], and they are traditional Yup'ik women. They were really elders and other women would look up to them as role models for how to be Yup'ik

women. I tried to set this tone of speaking Yugtun was not just okay but that it was what it was all about. They had to write in English because that was the medium for the institution and I had to give them feedback. But we would get started and get the ball rolling and then they would switch to Yugtun and carry on and I thought that was great. They bonded through that and apart from me but with my assistance.

PHD CANDIDATE AS MEDIATOR. As noted many times before, the PhD students were Alaska Native, but only two (Walkie Charles and Theresa Arevgaq John) were themselves Yup'ik. April Counceller was Alutiiq, a closely related Eskimo language/cultural group, and Hishinlai' "Kathy R. Sikorski" was Gwich'in, an Alaska Athabascan language/cultural group. Inclusion of Indigenous PhD students was part of a purposeful attempt to create a safe and welcoming environment for the teachers. As the following exchange illustrates, the doctoral students' personal knowledge of their own Indigenous languages and cultures allowed them to provide important near-peer support for the teachers.

MARLOW: The PhD students were another key element of the model. If we had gone into this blindly as four white academics with "all of the knowledge," without creating that space for the PhD students to be the mediators, the program would not have worked as well. Even when the PhD candidate didn't see him- or herself as a mediator, they were in that role. For example, for the most part April portrayed herself as "just another student" with the teachers. She also felt herself outsidered a bit, or outsidered herself a bit, because she wasn't Yup'ik, and she was younger than the teachers so she felt subordinate to them. Yet all of that comes together in a way that, when I asked the teachers, several of them said, "Oh, Patrick was so out to lunch, if April hadn't been there, none of this would have worked."

COLES-RITCHIE: Theresa was probably the closest match to the teachers themselves. She is Yup'ik, she speaks the language, she is a woman, she understands pedagogy, she's a professor, and she is their age or older. All of those things make her the ideal. She can relate to them and they can relate to her.

PARKER WEBSTER: And she knew most of the teachers personally and knew their families. For example, when she told me that [Name] was one of six sisters and when they get together they just have to be the "loudest" and they call each other out on things. Once I knew that, I knew I could just call [Name] out on things. That really changed my relationship with her.

MARLOW: And I know they spent a lot of time at Theresa's house in the summer. You would see a bunch of the teachers leaving campus in a hurry at lunch and you knew they were all going over to Theresa's to eat Native foods and just let loose. That was a really important safety valve for them.

COLES-RITCHIE: Walkie was an important mentor, too. It wasn't quite the same as with Theresa since he is a man, but [Name] told me what a great help he was by sharing his experiences, sharing articles and modeling his work. But I think it was even more important that he was able to conduct some of our meetings in Yugtun. That made a huge difference for [Name] in my GRC. And she said the same thing to Walkie about our summer class. "It was a good thing that you were there. I connected with you and you scaffolded it in a way that Marilee couldn't have done." That was huge in our group as well. I don't think all the students felt as strongly as she did, but that was a huge thing for her, and it is part of where she is in critiquing whitestream society and the impact the whitestream has had on schools, her own family and the language. Having Walkie there as a coinstructor was really important. There would have been a block if it had just been a white instructor and nobody else.

The PhD students were also important mentors for the faculty. Through them we the faculty were able to integrate Indigenous theories and methodologies into our courses, our own research, and most important into our understandings of the teachers and their context.

PARKER WEBSTER: Theresa and I were really able to team teach in a way that was really cool. She presented the Yup'ik epistemology and pedagogy and all of that, and I would present the Western concepts and Western literature and we would meet in the middle. So it was like, it was really an interesting way to work.

MARLOW: For me working with April really pulled my field of vision out quite a bit. She was so focused on hitting upon Indigenous methodologies and Indigenous researchers and Indigenous research in her thesis, and she resisted writing about Western theories and Western models even when they fit her data well.

> That dialogue really pushed us both. So by the time we sat down to really put the syllabus together for Language Policy and Planning, we had quite a bit of material on Indigenous methodologies and Indigenous theories that we could bring into the class. And I think that was another reason why the students connected so much to the class. And it has also worked out for my thinking about how language policy and planning research should be conducted.

Defining Success

Success for a project like this one can be defined in fairly simple, straightforward ways. The original grant narrative listed five goals, each with discrete, measurable outcomes. These goals may be further grouped into three broad categories: program completion, institutionalization, and capacity building. In terms of program completion, the grant proposal promised to graduate twenty MA or MEd students. In terms of institutionalization, it promised to establish the SLATE program and four GRCs. Finally, in terms of capacity building, it promised that all four PhD students would be eligible for promotion into tenure-track positions on graduation and that all the graduates would be eligible for leadership roles in community and school district programs. Furthermore, the proposal stated that all program graduates would be eligible to teach in programs offered by the University of Alaska Fairbanks (UAF). At the time of this writing, these goals have largely been achieved. The SLATE program is established, eighteen master's degree students have graduated, one former PhD student (John) has earned tenure, another former PhD student (Charles) has been promoted into a tenure-track position, a third former PhD student (Counceller) has moved into a term-funded position, and several other graduates have moved into leadership positions. Yet this straightforward assessment fails to capture both the depth of the stated goals and the breadth of the achievements.

PROGRAM COMPLETION. As discussed in Chapter 1, the time frame for degree completion was largely determined by the three-year grant funding cycle. Although many master's degrees have completion timelines, it is generally understood that the actual time for degree completion is variable and determined by a student's individual situation. However, for this project, the need to lead students to degree completion within the given time frame was crucial, because after the grant funding ran out, no further financial support would be available for students who depended on it.

SIEKMANN: For me, I just remember feeling a lot of pressure to get students through. To get them done on time. It was a three-year grant, but by the time they started the program in summer 2007, the teachers only had two years and a summer to complete their program. So we had to design everything to fit into seven semesters of summer-fall-spring, summer-fall-spring, and summer. So they really were under the gun the whole time. We all were.

Thus, the pressure to "get them done" was ever present and the sense of accomplishment in "getting them done" cannot be overestimated. As numerous earlier discussions and the following exchange demonstrate, the support provided by the GRCs was central to this accomplishment.

SIEKMANN: For me, there is success in just getting them done. Everyone who made it through the first summer session made it through to the end of the program and graduated. We all made it through to the end. That is one measure of success.

PARKER WEBSTER: Without the GRCs I don't think anyone would have finished in that amount of time. I mean, there are so many graduate students that are dangling out there because they wait until they are done with all their coursework to define the thesis or project. They finish the course work and suddenly it's "now you gotta do your thesis."

SIEKMANN: And we were aware of that history of distance graduate education, where people take course work and then [say] "Okay, I am done with my coursework, now I will think about my thesis." Changing that was an important part of the initial conversations when we decided to write the grant.

This pressure to "get them done" was further complicated by the fact that the teachers themselves had real lives. All continued to work full-time as teachers; all had family and community responsibilities, including important subsistence responsibilities unique to their own local Indigenous context.

PARKER WEBSTER: I also think it is important to recognize that this whole time issue is not just time for the program, for the coursework, but these women are teachers. You don't just clock out at three o'clock.

SIEKMANN: They were in school, but their lives continued. Whales were caught and people died. I know when I was in the villages it felt like time was a very different concept from being in Fairbanks and at the university.

COLES-RITCHIE: They had that full-time job and they also had other responsibilities in the community. In many ways, they are the real leaders and stalwarts of the community.

SIEKMANN: The commitment of these women was just amazing, and part of that is just who these women are. They are key people in their communities, and each one was kind of picked by their community to be in this program. So I think they really felt that responsibility to the community that helped select them. Can you imagine that? Having that responsibility on your shoulders?

INSTITUTIONALIZATION. The faculty recognized that as important as the individual success of the student is, individual successes do not largely alter how the university or academia in general function. Changes at these levels require the institutionalization of programs and ways of doing things. Accomplishing systemic change requires public recognition of the individual and group successes. As in all other elements of the project, grant timelines affected efforts toward institutionalization.

MARLOW: Strategically we had to demonstrate our success, and we had to use that success in order to institutionalize it. If you don't manage to institutionalize your success, then at some level you haven't succeeded. And institutionalizing that success is institutionalizing it at both the university and in the region our graduates are coming from.

PARKER WEBSTER: How do you accomplish that? How do you institutionalize it? Especially when you are dealing with grant funding cycles?

MARLOW: Institutionalizing the program at the university meant building a program that has status within the department and is recognized within the broader institution. It was not easy to get the linguistics program to accept a focus on language teaching, and I feel there may still be some tensions in the broader program over the status of the SLATE program. So we needed to create a rigorous program that graduated students who were doing meaningful research. The same goes for institutionalization in the region. The students needed to be doing meaningful research that could be useful and recognized in the region.

SIEKMANN: I think students that graduate from our program have a better idea about research than I did when I did my master's degree. And of course their research matters more than mine did. Their theses involve real-life applications that come from the real world. They aren't just coming up with an interesting question. Comparing their experience to my own, the quality that I produced, I think we have some wonderful examples.

Efforts toward institutionalization began as soon as the grant was awarded. Beginning in fall 2006, even before student applications were due, faculty started revising the existing MA in applied linguistics to include a second language acquisition teacher education focus. Once students began taking coursework, faculty used formal public presentations of student work (a poster session in summer 2007 and a formal student conference in summer 2008) in an effort to give the program a broad public presence on campus. These efforts were well received by both UAF faculty and administrators. However, as the following exchange highlights, these "performances" also created tension as several of the teachers questioned the legitimacy and need for public displays of their work. Even as the creation of this "public face" risked alienation of the teachers themselves, the public recognition of the teachers and their work made them academic players.

SIEKMANN: I want to talk a little more about the presentations we required the teachers to do at the end of each summer session. I know the summer presentations, at some level, were about the students and the students' developing experience in talking to other people and making presentations. But it seems that there was also a strategic attempt to give a public face to the program.

MARLOW: My rationale for pushing the students to do those presentations, really number one was that the students needed an experience of public presentation that went beyond standing up in front of their colleagues in the classroom. They needed to make that step. If their research is going to be out there, they need to be ready to present it. That said, I have to admit giving the program a public face and pushing for acceptance and permanence of the program at the university was a serious motivation.

SIEKMANN: I think the students may have reacted against that second motivation in some small way. I think they may have felt they were being presented, being used, being put on display to show how great we [the faculty] are.

PARKER WEBSTER: When we were doing the IRB [Institutional Review Board][1] protocol to get approval for research on the program, [Name]'s hand goes up and she asks, "So does that mean you are going to do research on us?" And that is exactly how some of the teachers felt.

COLES-RITCHIE: There wasn't just a fear that they wouldn't do a good job, but there was also a resistance to being put on display.

SIEKMANN: The poster child Native person. I just wanted to bring that up, because I think there was that sense. We invited the dean, and we invited everyone up the chain. And that is important. And I am doing a lot of that with my grant [supporting materials development for the Yup'ik classroom]. I get newspaper reporters in, and get things in the newspaper, because it is important.

PARKER WEBSTER: And why? Why was it important?

SIEKMANN: I don't think I saw it so much for SLATE so maybe I was resisting, I don't know. The reason I do it now for the grant I am currently responsible for is because I talked to the teachers and I said we need to get these stories out there. We need to let people know what we are doing . . . so that people can't dismiss what you are saying . . . If there is a newspaper article in one of the local papers, the *Tundra Drums*, about what we are doing, people will read that and be like, "Oh look, there are these teachers, and they are doing meaningful work." That's part of changing the perceptions of the institution about what Indigenous students can do. That is how I have taken it, that is how I am using that idea of putting you in a position of power, of using the system to put you in a position of power that cannot be argued with in the same way. Once it is published, people can't simply say "Yeah, but you are only a teacher and there is this other stuff out there that is so much more important."

PARKER WEBSTER: You are making them academic players.

CAPACITY BUILDING. Building capacity for local leadership was an important goal of the project. As noted, a goal of the original grant proposal defined capacity building as the eligibility of all four PhD students to be promoted into tenure-track positions on graduation, as well as the eligibility of all project graduates for leadership roles in community and school district programs. As Siekmann explains, as the project reached its conclusion, this goal above all others became central: "The goal that really matters, and I didn't really get this when we were writing the grant, is building capacity for local leadership—handing over the baton to the PhD students and the teachers. That is what it is really about for me now, giving people the tools to chart their own course."

At the school and district levels, SLATE graduates have begun to take on leadership roles, as Marlow tells us:

> The big step for me is ultimately these "students" become themselves the leaders, the teachers in different contexts . . . that they are pushing it forward themselves in some format. Which is why I am so thrilled that Sabine is continuing to work with a cohort of SLATE graduates on the materials development project, and I am so thrilled that [Name 1] has moved into the district office and I am so thrilled that [Name 2] is talking about going on and getting her principal's license, and [Name 3], after resisting it for so long, is now saying, "I should be involved in planning for my school and helping to decide what kind of language program we should have." So all of those things are part of moving forward. And part of that is pushing their buttons a little bit because it does require that they say, in a culturally appropriate way, that "I do have something to say, I do have a responsibility here, I should take on this leadership responsibility." To use their phrase, they are becoming aware [*ellangluni*].

Yet as the following exchange demonstrates, predefined/institutionalized leadership roles (e.g., tenure at the university; administrative positions within a school district) are only platforms from which individuals may (or may not) choose to make positive change. Thus, while obtaining the platform is important, obtaining the tools necessary to transform that platform is essential.

SIEKMANN: It is really about giving people the tools to pursue their own agenda.

PARKER WEBSTER: You're talking about research as pedagogy. That is huge. That is more than teaching people how to do research. It is a whole pedagogical stance. A pedagogy of research. That is what I would like to talk about at some point. It is very different from a methods course.

COLES-RITCHIE: What and how do you construct a program that

the goal is for research to continue? What pedagogical tools are necessary that students really do go out and say, "We know research is a process. We know that. Now, we can continue and decide what we want to research and how to do it"?

MARLOW: And it isn't just, "Yeah, I got my degree. Now I am done!"

COLES-RITCHIE: A lot of times, I think for people who get their master's, they think they are done and then they continue teaching. They do not understand that this research is a tool for improving their teaching or for changing local practice. But I think they [these teachers] get that they are not done. This is the beginning, not the end.

Just as getting the degree is only a beginning and not an end for the teachers, so "getting them done" must be a beginning and not an end for the faculty. As the following discussion reveals, commitment to systemic change cannot be limited by grant funding cycles or degree completion. Systemic change requires sustained effort, which in turn requires multiple generations of actors working for that change.

PARKER WEBSTER: This has been problematic for teacher research for decades. Let's do teacher research. Yippee. We get a master's and do teacher research. And once it is done, there is no teacher research. So how can teachers ever have a voice theoretically, pedagogically?

SIEKMANN: And they need further support after the master's. Patrick and I both have projects in the region, and in both cases we are working with our graduates and bringing in other teachers and trying to take those next steps.

PARKER WEBSTER: Okay, I am going to throw this out because this is, I think, a problem. When you are relying on federal grants and not making something self-sustaining, you are always going to have the systemic problem of things falling off the face of the Earth. It is a social problem. It is about systemic change. People have been talking about this for longer than I can remember.

SIEKMANN: Yeah. There is a problem with relying on money that is time limited. Which is one of the problems we had with your [Parker Webster's and Coles-Ritchie's] positions. Those positions were grant funded. They ended when the grant ended. I mean, how can you really change a program and add courses and add a whole new strand within the MA without having faculty that are paid in the long term to do that? And that is always a struggle. But I think it is in part in the way you approach it. You don't just look at it in terms of "it all hinges on me and if I don't do it then nobody will." It is about engendering that role in others: You [the teachers] are the ones that are driving this and here are some things, some tools, that would allow you to get in the driver's seat and drive the truck down the road. Rather than just saying, "Okay, this is the end point. Everybody get off the bus."

PARKER WEBSTER: I totally agree with all of it. And I have seen things . . . one thing that gives me hope about this type of group, because I have been involved in teacher research for a long, long time. And all of these principles, I hear them all the time, and I hear groups say they are going to stay together and publish, and I have been a part of that. And one by one by one, the group falls away. But I think the potential here to keep this together and ongoing is that there is so much at stake. And there is a culture that unites, there is a social justice cause that unites these teachers.

MARLOW: I think, in the end, life is life, and people will spin off. So at that point it has to become a self-generating, self-perpetuating group. These folks are only a first generation. They are not *it*. They are generation 1. And if we can figure out ways for them to foster generation 2, and we might have to be involved in fostering generation 2. But hopefully by the time we get to generation 3, 4, and 5 they won't need us in supporting roles. They will have all of those skills and all of the authority for themselves.

Time, Trust, and Support: Implications for Maintaining a Community of Research and Practice

In the conclusion to their discussion of mentoring (Chapter 2) Parker Webster and Siekmann remind us that mentoring within the SLATE project relied on the creation of a "third space" that brought together Indigenous and Western epistemologies and methodologies. Although this third space was "sometimes filled with anxiety and incomprehension, it was also a space for creativity where new knowledge and new relationships were forged." Now, at the end of the project, we look back at the elements needed to create an environment conducive to the creation of this third space, and we find the recurrent themes of time, trust, and support.

As Siekmann implied in our discussion of program completion, time may refer to external and internal (self-imposed) pressures to "get them [the teachers] done." In this sense, time is ultimately a Western metaphor (e.g., time is money, don't waste time) and reflects both the Western point of view of the faculty (the authors of these conversations) as well as the Western view of the academy and the institutions the faculty represent. In this sense, the metaphor of time represents the externally imposed requirements of the funding agency (a three-year grant from the US Department of Education) and the university (the discrete requirements of a degree program). At the same time, as Siekmann reminds us, in the village "it felt like time was a very different concept." In this frame, where survival depends on the coming of the seasons and with them the subsistence opportunities the people have relied on for centuries, time is less linear and more spatial. This "village time" is not the time of the Western clock or calendar but the open-ended time that comes when the fish arrive and ends when enough fish are cut and dried for the year or when the "time" for another subsistence activity demands one's immediate attention.

Support, for us, refers to the structure provided by a defined degree program or course syllabus; the physical support of grant funds needed to provide travel, housing, meals, books, and other physical needs of students in a degree program; as well as the less tangible but no less important interpersonal support provided by people working toward a common goal.

We see trust as a way of characterizing interpersonal relationships. Trust is established when two people are willing and able to rely on each other to fulfill certain roles and obligations. What those roles and obligations are must be negotiated by the people seeking the relationship and ultimately depend on the "physical and sociocultural context and the social and cultural identities of those involved in the relationship" (Chapter 2). So, as Siekmann says, "there wasn't trust between us," because the history of Indigenous research meant that it was not sufficient for us as faculty to simply adopt the role of faculty and for the teachers to adopt the role of graduate students. All of us involved in the SLATE program had to also adopt the roles of coresearcher, coactivist, friend, and advocate to overcome that history.

The diagram in Figure 7.1 is our attempt to represent the relationships between these themes as they interact to create a hospitable ecosystem for our community of research and practice. In this diagram, time is a constant pressure on the exterior of the circle. As discussed earlier, this pressure has numerous sources: grant pressure, institutional pressure, and subsistence pressure, to name just a few. Support refers to the circle itself. It is

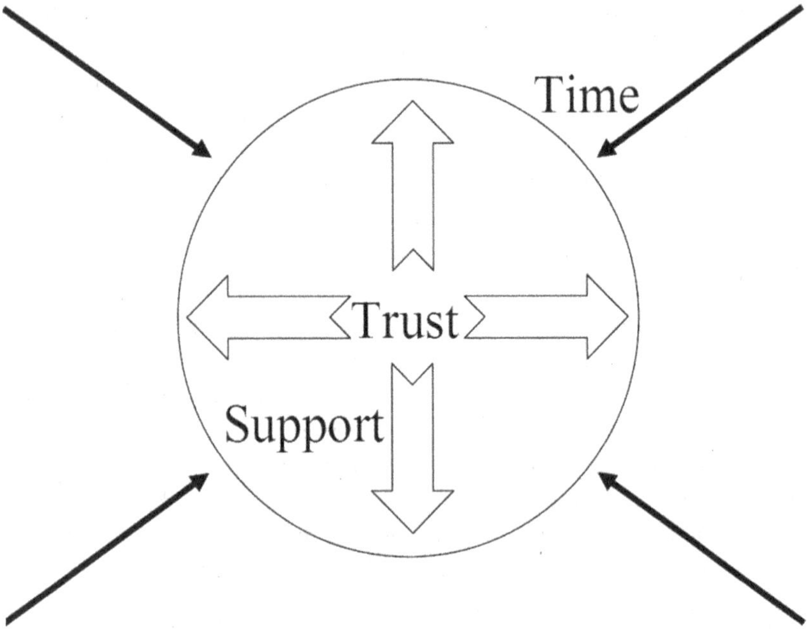

Figure 7.1. Relationship between time, trust, and support

relatively thin and potentially permeable or breakable. For the supports (both structural and interpersonal) to function, for the circle to be maintained, trust between all parties involved in the community we seek to create must be established and maintained. Failure to establish or maintain this trust means that the external pressure represented by time will push inward on the circle and undermine the supports that actors have put into place.

When the ecosystem represented by the diagram is healthy, when we are able to put sufficient supports in place, and when we are able to foster trust between all the actors, only then will we be able to create sufficient space to both create and maintain a community of research and practice.

Notes

1. The Institutional Review Board at the University of Alaska Fairbanks (UAF) is responsible for approving, monitoring, and reviewing all human subjects research at UAF. It is designed to guarantee and protect the rights and protections of all research participants.

Epilogue

Although this volume focuses exclusively on the Second Language Acquisition Teacher Education (SLATE) project, this program is neither the beginning nor the end of our story. Partnerships like those that were at the heart of the effort described in this book do not happen overnight; they take years to develop. In fact, many of the relationships and mechanisms supporting our collaboration were first established in 2002 with the Yup'ik Language Institute, the first in a series of efforts funded by the US Department of Education (see Table E.1). As discussed in Marlow and Siekmann (forthcoming), these earlier efforts were the prequel to the SLATE story. For now, however, we focus on the sequel.

As discussed in Chapter 7, although program completion was a concrete and measurable outcome of the SLATE grant, we see this measure of success as only a step toward the ultimate goals of capacity building and fostering local control in language programming. As Siekmann told us in Chapter 7, "The goal that really matters . . . is building capacity for local leadership—handing over the baton to the PhD students and the teachers."

At the university level, handing over that baton can most easily be established by Indigenous faculty members moving into senior positions. In terms of this goal, the SLATE doctoral graduates have been extraordinarily successful. Dr. Theresa Arevgaq John was tenured and promoted to associate professor of Alaska Native Studies at University of Alaska Fairbanks (UAF) in 2010; Dr. Walkie Charles was hired into a tenure-track position within the Alaska Native Language program in 2011 and is currently chairing a committee of Yup'ik faculty (including Dr. John) reviewing and

Table E.1. Related Projects

Title	*Yup'ik Language Institute (YLI)*	*Yupiit Nakmiin Qaneryaraat (YNQ)*	*Preparing Teachers of Yup'ik Language & Culture (PTYLC)*	*Second Language Acquisition & Teacher Education (SLATE)*	*Piciryaramta Elicungcallra (PE)*
Duration	2002–2006	2005–2009	2008–2012	2006–2010	2009–2012
Grant identification	US Department of Education, Alaska Native Education, #S356A020049; #S356A050047; #S356A080043; #S356A060055; #S356A090066				
Partnered organizations*	University of Alaska Fairbanks: Alaska Native Language Center, School of Education, Linguistics Program, Kuskokwim Campus, and Bristol Bay Campus School Districts: Lower Kuskokwim, Lower Yukon, Kuspuk, and Southwest Regional Alaska Native Organizations: Association of Village Council Presidents				
Project Goals	Establish relevant pre-baccalaureate and postcertification programs at UAF Graduate students from relevant programs Establish career ladders in partner districts	Establish baccalaureate (BA) program in Yup'ik Continue support for students in relevant programs	Deliver Yup'ik BA and establish bridge from BA to teacher certification Recruit 9 part-time/distance and 6 full-time students to work on AAS and BA degrees	Establish SLATE graduate emphasis in existing MA in applied linguistics program Graduate up to 20 MA/MEd focusing on Yup'ik and/or English language education Graduate 4 Alaska Native PhD students	Develop technology-infused materials for Yup'ik-medium schools

*Not all partnered organizations participated in all projects. For more detail see Marlow & Siekmann, forthcoming.

revising existing UAF programs. Likewise, Dr. April Counceller was hired into a term assistant professor position at Kodiak College, a branch campus of the University of Alaska Anchorage, in 2011 and has been charged with coordinating the new Alutiiq Studies program there.

As in any graduate program, the teachers and the PhD students contributed to the academic conversation through their theses. Unlike most such programs, however, we find evidence that SLATE theses are also contributing to the local conversation. As Marlow and Siekmann (forthcoming) explain, the superintendent of at least one partnered school district has taken it upon himself to read each thesis. Privately, this same person said that these teachers were likely to transform local school practice in ways that none of us could yet predict.

Given the reception the teachers' theses have received, it is perhaps not surprising that at least some of the SLATE graduates are looking for ways to move into positions of authority and continue engaging in meaningful local projects. Patrick Marlow and April Counceller (Chapter 6) reported that two SLATE graduates "now work in the Curriculum and Instruction department, where they are responsible for leading the implementation of a new K–6 Yugtun-English dual language program intended to replace the early transition K–3 Yugtun programs in place in the region since the early 1970s." These same graduates are also working with Marlow and other collaborators investigating the effect of high-stakes testing on Yugtun medium education (2011), a project funded by Alaska's Institute for Social and Economic Research. Sabine Siekmann and Hishinlai' "Kathy R. Sikorski" (Chapter 3) reported that eight SLATE graduates are working on the Piciryaramta Elicungcallra (Teaching Our Way of Life through Our Language) project, a US Department of Education grant to develop technology-infused materials for the Yugtun medium classroom. In this context Cathy Moses, a teacher involved in the Piciryaramta Elicungcallra project, explained that it is the "SLATE sisters" that her district now turns to for leadership on questions of language and culture.

However, as the following extended excerpt from Marlow and Siekmann (forthcoming) demonstrates, the teachers still face many uphill battles.

> When one SLATE graduate was abruptly told by her district office that the K–3 immersion program in which she taught would be shifting to include 50% English instruction per day, the teacher and her community were stunned. It appeared that the district decision had been made on the assumption that seat time in English would

improve NCLB [No Child Left Behind] mandated test scores. As the district had not consulted the school or its teachers—two of whom had graduated from the SLATE program—there was no time to argue the point from either an academic or personal research perspective. Past experience tells us that this could have been the end of the whole matter. The district office had made its decision. The teachers, however, had something else in mind. . . . They made plans to attend the final school board meeting of the year—a decision which required the chartering of a small plane for the day—to present their case. Fortunately, the school board reversed the decision by the district office.

Bass: What helped me was having you [Siekmann] as a sounding board. . . . And I think I wouldn't have gone as far as I [did] without your advice and input. . . . Because . . . I wouldn't have had the resources I have . . . all the research papers—what research says about second language acquisition and language development and so on. So, it helped *me* having gone through the SLATE program and having been involved in materials development.

As we stated in Chapter 7, "Just as getting the degree is only a beginning and not an end for the teachers, so 'getting them done' must be a beginning and not an end for the faculty." In addition to the efforts already described, two recent grant proposals are worth mentioning here. The first, Improving Alaska Native Education through Computer Assisted Language Learning (funded by the US Department of Education's Alaska Native Education program), will engage SLATE PhD graduates as faculty advisers to additional cohorts of teachers and Alaska Native doctoral candidates. The second, Teacher Certification for Yup'ik-English Dual Language Programs (to be submitted in spring 2013 to the US Department of Education) would engage the SLATE teachers as university faculty to educate the next generation of certified Yugtun-medium teachers.

We believe Barbara Amos-Andrew, one of the SLATE teachers, summed up not only her involvement in these and other efforts but also those of her "SLATE sisters" as well as the faculty and PhD graduates when she said: "I want to do more. I want to do more. And actually you know what I keep thinking of? It keeps coming into my head—continue doing research" (Marlow & Siekmann forthcoming).

References

Abedi, J. (2004). The No Child Left Behind Act and English language learners: Assessment and accountability issues. *Educational Researcher* 33(1), 4–14.

Abley, M. (2003). *Spoken here: Travels among threatened languages.* Houghton Mifflin.

Alton, T. (1998). Federal education policies and Alaska Native languages since 1867. Doctoral dissertation, University of Alaska Fairbanks.

Amos-Andrew, B. (2010). Kuiggluk speech community. Master's thesis, University of Alaska Fairbanks. Proquest 1485998.

Angiak-Bond, A. (2010). Becoming aware as a parent, schoolteacher, and community member. Master's thesis, University of Alaska Fairbanks. Proquest 1486000.

Appel, G. A., & Lantolf, J. P. (1994). Theoretical framework: An introduction to Vygotskian approaches to second language research. In J. P. Lantolf & G. A. Appel (Eds.), *Vygotskian approaches to second language research* (pp. 1–32). New York: Ablex Publishing.

Arnold, N., & Ducate, L. (Eds.) (2011). *Present and future promises of CALL: From theory and research to new directions in language teaching.* San Marcos, TX: CALICO Publications.

Atkinson, D. R., Neville, H., & Casas, A. (1991). The mentorship of ethnic minorities in professional psychology. *Professional Psychology: Research and Practice* 22, 336–38.

Atweh, B., Kemmis, S., & Weeks, P. (Eds.) (1998). *Action research in practice: Partnership for social justice in education.* London: Routledge.

Baldauf, R. B., Jr. (2005). Micro language planning. In P. Bruthiaux, D. Atkinson, W. G. Eggington, W. Grabe, & V. Ramanathan (Eds.), *Studies in applied linguistics* (pp. 227–39). Clevedon, UK: Multilingual Matters.

Baldauf, R. B., Jr. (2006). Rearticulating the case for micro language planning in a language ecology context. *Current Issues in Language Planning* 7(2–3), 147–70.

Barnhardt, R., & Kawagley, A. O. (2005). Indigenous knowledge systems and Alaska Native ways of knowing. *Anthropology & Education Quarterly* 36(1), 8–23.

Bass, A. S. (2010). Bridging home and school: Factors that contribute to multiliteracies development in a Yup'ik kindergarten classroom. Master's thesis, University of Alaska Fairbanks. Proquest 1485999.

Battiste, M. (2002). *Indigenous knowledge and pedagogy in First Nations education: A literature review with recommendations.* Ottawa: Indian and Northern Affairs Canada.

Baumann, J. F., & Duffy, A. M. (2001). Teacher-research methodology: Themes, variations, and possibilities. *Reading Teacher 54*, 608–615.

Belz, J. A., & Thorne, S. L. (Eds). (2006). *Internet-mediated intercultural foreign language education.* Boston: Heinle & Heinle.

Boal, A. (1979). *Theatre of the oppressed,* trans. Charles A. McBride. New York: Urizen.

Bray, T., & Killion, T. (1994). *Reckoning with the dead: The Larsen Bay Repatriation and the Smithsonian Institution.* Washington, DC: Smithsonian Institution Press.

Brayboy, B. (2005). Toward a critical race theory in education. *Urban Review* 37(5), 425–45.

Brayboy, B., & Maughan, E. (2009). Indigenous knowledges and the story of the bean. *Harvard Educational Review* 79(1), 1–21.

Burnaby, B., & Reyhner, J. (Eds.). (2002). *Indigenous languages across the community.* Flagstaff: Center for Excellence in Education, Northern Arizona University.

Cajete, G. (2008). Sites of strength in Indigenous research. In M. Villegas, S. R. Neugebauer, & K. R. Venegas (Eds.), *Indigenous knowledge and education* (pp. 204–7). Cambridge, MA: Harvard Educational Review.

Calkins, L. (1994). *The art of teaching writing.* Portsmouth, NH: Heinemann.

Calvet, L.-J. (1998). *Language wars and linguistic politics.* New York: Oxford University Press.

Carspecken, P. F. (1996). *Critical ethnography in educational research: A theoretical and practical guide.* New York: Routledge.

Cazden, C. B. (1988). *Classroom discourse: The language of teaching and learning.* Portsmouth, NH: Heinemann Educational Books.

Chan, A. W. (2008). Mentoring ethnic minority, pre-doctoral students: An analysis of key mentor practices. *Mentoring & Tutoring: Partnership in Learning* 1(3), 263–77.

Chapelle, C. A. (2001). *Computer applications in second language acquisitions: Foundations for teaching, testing and research.* Cambridge: Cambridge University Press.

Charmaz, K. (2000). Grounded theory: Objectivist and constructivist methods. In N. K. Denzin & Y. S. Lincoln (Eds.), *Handbook of qualitative research* (2nd ed., pp. 509–35). Thousand Oaks, CA: Sage.

Cochran-Smith, M., & Lytle, S. L. (1993). *Inside/outside: Teacher research and knowledge.* New York: Teachers College Press.

Coles-Ritchie, M., & Charles, W. (2011). Indigenizing assessment using community funds of knowledge: A critical action research study. *Journal of American Indian Education* 20(3), 24–39.

Cooper, R. L. (1989). *Language planning and social change.* Cambridge: Cambridge University Press.

Counceller, A. G. L. (2010). *Niugneliyukut* (we are making new words): A community philosophy of language revitalization. Doctoral dissertation, University of Alaska Fairbanks.

Crawford, J. (2004). *Educating English learners: Language diversity in the classroom* (5th ed.). Los Angeles: Bilingual Education Services.

Crystal, D. (2000). *Language death*. Cambridge: Cambridge University Press.

Daniels, H. (1994). *Literature circles: Voice and choice in the student-centered classroom*. Portland, ME: Stenhouse.

Daniels, H. (2001). *Literature circles: Voice and choice in book clubs and reading groups*. Portland, ME: Stenhouse.

Darder, A. (2008). *The critical pedagogy reader* (2nd ed.). New York: Routledge.

Delgado, R., & Stefancic, J. (2001). *Critical race theory: An introduction*. New York: New York University Press.

Deloria, V., Jr. (1991). *Indian education in America*. Boulder, CO: Kivaki Press.

Deloria, V., Jr., & Wildcat, D. R. (2001). *Power and place: Indian education in America*. Golden, CO: Fulcrum Resources.

Dewey, J. (1916). *Democracy and education: An introduction to the philosophy of education*. New York: Macmillan.

Deyhle, D., & McCarty, T. L. (2007). Beatrice Medicine and the anthropology of education: Legacy and vision for critical race/critical language research and practice. *Anthropology & Education Quarterly* 38(3), 209–20.

Donato, R. (1994). Collective scaffolding in second language learning. In J. P. Lantolf & G. A. Appel (Eds.), *Vygotskian approaches to second language research* (pp. 173–93). Norwood, NJ: Ablex.

Duchene, A., & Heller, M. (2007). Discourses of endangerment: Sociolinguistics, globalization and social order. In A. Duchene & M. Heller (Eds.), *Discourses of endangerment: Interest and ideology in the defense of languages* (pp. 1–13). London: Continuum.

Erben, T., & Sarieva, I. (2008). *CALLing all foreign language teachers: Computer-assisted language learning in the classroom*. New York: Eye on Education.

Fishman, J. A. (1974). Language modernization and planning in comparison with other types of national modernization and planning. In J. A. Fishman (Ed.), *Advances in language planning* (pp. 79–102). The Hague: Mouton.

Fishman, J. A. (1991). *Reversing language shift*. Clevedon, UK: Multilingual Matters.

Fishman, J. A. (Ed). (2001). *Can threatened languages be saved?* Clevedon, UK: Multilingual Matters.

Foley, D., & Valenzuela, A. (2000). Critical ethnography: The politics of collaboration. In N. K. Denzin & Y. S. Lincoln (Eds.), *Handbook of qualitative research* (2nd ed., pp. 217–34). Thousand Oaks, CA: Sage.

Fotos, S., & Browne, C. M. (Eds.) (2004). *New perspectives on CALL for second language classroom*. Mahwah, NJ: Lawrence Erlbaum.

Freire, P. (2000). *Pedagogy of the oppressed, 30th anniversary edition*, trans. M. B. Ramos. New York: Continuum (original work published 1968).

Gallas, K. (1995). *Talking their way into science*. New York: Teacher's College Press.

Gee, J. P. (1992). *The social mind: Language, ideology, and social practice*. New York: Bergin & Garvey.

Gee, J. P. (1996). *Social linguistics and literacies: Ideology in discourses* (2nd ed.). London: Taylor & Francis.

Gee, J.P. (2007). *An introduction to discourse analysis: Theory and method* (2nd ed.). New York: Routledge.

Gegeo, D., & Watson-Gegeo, K. (1999). Adult education, language change, and issues of identity and authenticity in Kwara'ae (Solomon Islands). *Anthropology & Education Quarterly* 30(1), 22–36.

Genesee, F. (1987). *Learning through two languages: Studies of immersion and bilingual education*. Rowley, MA: Newbury.

Glaser, B., & Strauss, A. (1967). *The discovery of grounded theory*. Chicago: Aldine.

Gonzalez, N., Moll, L., & Amanti, C. (2005). *Funds of knowledge: Theorizing practices in households, communities, and classrooms*. Mahwah, NJ: Lawrence Erlbaum.

Grand, S. (2000). American Indian identity and intellectualism: The quest for a new red pedagogy. *International Journal of Qualitative Studies in Education 13*(4), 343–59.

Green, J. R. (2010). Investigating a Yup'ik immersion program: What determines success? Master's thesis, University of Alaska Fairbanks. Proquest 1486001.

Grenoble, L. A., & Whaley, L. J. (Eds.). (1998). *Endangered languages*. Cambridge: Cambridge University Press.

Gutierrez, K. D., Asato, J., Pacheco, M., Moll, L. C., Olson, K., Horng, E. L., Ruiz, R., García, E., & McCarty, T. L. (2002). "Sounding American": The consequences of new reforms on English language learners. *Reading Research Quarterly* 37(3), 328–43.

Gutierrez, K. D., Baquedano-Lopez, P., Alvarez, H., & Chiu, M. M. (1999). Building a culture of collaboration through hybrid language practices. *Theory into Practice* 38(2), 87–94.

Habermas, J. (1987). *The theory of communicative action: Lifeworld and system: A critique of functionalist reason*, trans. T. McCarthy. Boston: Beacon Press (original work published 1981).

Halliday, M. A. K. (1975). *Learning how to mean*. London: Edward Arnold.

Harjo, J., & Bird, G. (1997). Introduction. In J. Harjo & G. Bird (Eds.), *Reinventing the enemy's language: Contemporary Native women's writings of North America* (pp. 19-31). New York: Norton.

Haugen, E. (1959). Planning for a standard language in Norway. *Anthropological Linguistics 1*(3), 8–21.

Heath, S. B. (1983). *Ways with words: Language, life, and work in communities and classrooms*. New York: Cambridge University Press.

Heath, S. B. (1986). Sociocultural contexts of language development. In *Beyond language: Social and cultural factors in schooling language minority students* (pp. 143–86). Sacramento: California State Department of Education, Bilingual Education Office.

Hendrickson, K. I. (2010). Authentic assessment in action: The challenges, successes and discoveries made in a fifth grade classroom. Master's thesis, University of Alaska Fairbanks. Proquest 1486002.

Herr, K., & Anderson, G. (2005). *The action research dissertation: A guide for students and faculty*. London: Sage.

Hinton, L., & Hale, K. (Eds.). (2001.) *The green book of language revitalization in practice: Toward a sustainable world*. San Diego: Academic Press.

Hoffman, J. (2010). A parent's choice. Master's thesis, University of Alaska Fairbanks. Proquest 1486003.

Holmberg, Q. (2010). Yupik kindergartners' funds of knowledge. Unpublished master's project, University of Alaska Fairbanks.

hooks, b. (1994). *Teaching to transgress: Education as the practice of freedom*. New York: Routledge.

Huffman, B., & Sloat, T. (2004). *Berry magic*. Anchorage: Alaska Northwest Books.

Ignace, M. B. (1999). *Handbook for aboriginal language program planning in British Columbia*. North Vancouver: First Nations Education Steering Committee.

Jacobson, S. A. (1998). *Yup'ik dialect atlas and study*. Fairbanks: Alaska Native Language Center.

Johnson, R. K., & Swain, M. (Eds.). (1997.) *Immersion education: International perspectives*. Cambridge: Cambridge University Press.

Johnson, W. B. (2006). *On being a mentor: A guide for higher education faculty*. Mahwah, NJ: Lawrence Erlbaum.

Johnson, W. B. (2008). Are advocacy, mutuality, and evaluation incompatible mentoring functions? *Mentoring & Tutoring: Partnership in Learning 16*(1), 31–44.

Kaplan, R. B., & Baldauf, R. B., Jr. (1997). *Language planning from practice to theory*. Clevedon, UK: Multilingual Matters.

Karp, S. (2003). Let them eat tests: NCLB and federal educational policy. In L. Christensen & S. Karp (Eds.), *Rethinking school reform: Views from the classroom*. Milwaukee, WI: Rethinking Schools Publication.

Kavanaugh, E. (2010). Writing workshops: A sheltered instructional approach. Unpublished master's project, University of Alaska Fairbanks.

Kemmis, S., & McTaggart, R. (2000). Participatory action research. In N. K. Denzin & Y. S. Lincoln (Eds.), *Handbook of qualitative research* (2nd ed., pp. 567–605). Thousand Oaks, CA: Sage.

Kincheloe, J. (2008). *Critical pedagogy primer*. New York: Peter Lang.

Kipp, D. (2000). *Encouragement, guidance, insights, and lessons learned for Native language activists developing their own tribal language programs*. Browning, MT: Piegan Institute.

Kram, K. E. (1985). *Mentoring at work: Developmental relationship in organizational life*. Glenview, IL: Scott Foresman.

Krashen, S. D. (1981). *Second language acquisition and second language learning*. Oxford: Pergamon.

Krauss, M. E. (1980). *Alaska Native languages: Past, present and future*. Fairbanks: Alaska Native Language Center.

Krauss, M. E. (1992). The world's languages in crisis. *Language* 68(1), 4–10.

Krauss, M. E. (1997). Indigenous languages of the north: A report on their present state. In H. Shoji & J. Janhunen (Eds.), *Northern minority languages: Problems of survival. Senri Ethnological Studies 44*, 1–34. Osaka, Japan: National Museum of Ethnology.

Kress, G. (2000). Multimodality. In B. Cope & M. Kalantzis (Eds.), *Multiliteracies: Literacy learning and the design of social futures* (pp. 182–202), New York: Routledge.

Lantolf, J. P. (2000). Introducing sociocultural theory. In J. P. Lantolf (Ed.), *Sociocultural theory and second language learning* (pp. 1–26). Oxford: Oxford University Press.

Lantolf, J., & Thorne, S. L. (2006). *Sociocultural theory and the genesis of second language development*. Oxford: Oxford University Press.

Lave, J., & Wegner, E. (1991). *Situated learning: Legitimate peripheral participation*. New York: Cambridge University Press.

Lazaruk, W. (2007). Linguistic, academic, and cognitive benefits of French immersion. *Canadian Modern Language Review* 63, 605–28.

Lipka, J., Sharp, N., Adams, B., & Sharp, F. (2007). Creating third space for authentic biculturalism: Examples for math in a cultural context. *Journal of American Indian Education 46*, 94–115.

Lipka, J., Sharp, N., Brenner, B., Yanez, E., & Sharp, F. (1995). The relevance of culturally based curriculum and instruction: The case of Nancy Sharp. *Journal of American Indian Education 44*(3), 31–54.

Lomawaima, K. T., & McCarty, T. L. (2002). When tribal sovereignty challenges democracy: American Indian education and the democratic ideal. *American Educational Research Journal* 39(2), 279–305.

Lomawaima, K. T., & McCarty, T. L. (2006). The strengths of Indigenous education: Overturning myths about Indian learners. In *To remain an Indian: Lessons in democracy from a century of Native American education*. New York: Teachers College Press.

Long, M. H. (1991). Focus on form: A design feature in language teaching methodology. In K. de Bot, R. B. Ginsberg, & C. Kramsch (Eds.), *Foreign language research in cross-cultural perspective* (pp. 39–52). Amsterdam: John Benjamins.

Luke, A. (2000). Critical literacy in Australia: A matter of context and standpoint. *Journal of Adolescent and Adult Literacy* 43(5), 448–61.

Marlow, P. E. (2004). Bilingual education, legislative intent, and language maintenance in Alaska. *Proceedings of the 8th Foundation for Endangered Languages conference*. Barcelona: Institut d'Estudis Catalans.

Marlow, P. E., & Counceller, A. G. L. (2008, November). Reconciling tensions: Co-creating ownership in community action research. Paper presented at the annual meeting of the American Anthropological Association, San Francisco.

Marlow, P. E., & Counceller, A. G. L. (2009, March). I am the voice: Personal agency and power through language planning. Paper presented at the annual meeting of the American Association of Applied Linguistics, Denver.

Marlow, P. E., & Siekmann, S. (forthcoming). Changing the conversation. Promise and vulnerability in Alaska Native language revitalization. *Journal of American Indian Education.*

Marlow, P. E., Wyman, L., Andrew, F., Augustine, A., Crow, R., Miller, G., Nicholai, R., Rearden, N., & Winkelman, V. (2011, November). Local policy makers: Fostering understanding in language planning. Paper presented at the annual Language Education and Diversity Conference, Auckland, NZ.

Martin, K. (2008). The intersection of aboriginal knowledges, aboriginal literacies and new learning pedagogy for aboriginal students. In A. Healy (Ed.), *Multiliteracies and diversity in education: New pedagogies for expanding landscapes* (pp. 58–81). South Melbourne, Victoria: Oxford University Press.

Math in a Cultural Context. (n.d.). Lessons learned from Yup'ik Eskimo Elder's project. Retrieved June 12, 2011, from http://www.uaf.edu/mcc.

McCarty, T. L. (2003). Revitalising Indigenous languages in homogenizing times. *Comparative Education* 39(2), 319–47.

McCarty, T. L., & Watahomigie, L. J. (1999). Community-based indigenous language education in the USA. In S. May (Ed.), *Indigenous community-based education* (pp. 79–96). Clevedon, UK: Multilingual Matters.

McHenry, T. (2002, May). Words as big as the screen: Native American languages and the Internet. *Language Learning & Technology* 6(2), 102–15.

McLaren, P. (2007). *Critical pedagogy: Where are we now?* New York: Peter Lang.

McNiff, J., & Whitehead, J. (2006). *All you need to know about action research.* London: Sage.

Meskill, C. (2005). Triadic scaffolds: Tools for teaching English language learners with computers. *Language Learning Technology* 8(4), 46–59.

Michael, V. E. (2010). Can we remain Yup'ik in these contemporary times? Master's thesis, University of Alaska Fairbanks. Proquest 148604.

Mills, G. (2003). *Action research: A guide for the teacher researcher.* Columbus, OH: Prentice Hall.

Moses, C. (2010). Focus on form in writing in a third grade Yugtun classroom. Master's thesis, University of Alaska Fairbanks. Proquest 1486005.

Mullen, C. A. (2005). *Mentorship primer.* New York: Peter Lang.

Mullen, C. A., Cox, M. D., Boettcher, C. K., & Adoue, D. S. (2000). *Breaking the circle of one: Redefining mentorship in the lives and writings of educators.* New York: Peter Lang.

Narayan, U. (1988). Working together across difference: Some considerations on emotions and political practice. *Hypatia: A Journal of Feminist Philosophy* 3(2), 31–47.

Nelson-Barber, S., & Trumball, E. (2007). Making assessment practices valid for Indigenous American students. *Journal of American Indian Education* 46(3), 132–47.

Nettle, D., & S. Romaine (2000). *Vanishing voices: The extinction of the world's languages.* New York: Oxford University Press.

New London Group. (1996). A pedagogy of multiliteracies: Designing social futures. *Harvard Educational Review* 66(1), 60–92.

New London Group. (2000). A pedagogy of multiliteracies: Designing social futures. In B. Cope & M. Kalantzis (Eds.), *Multiliteracies: Literacy learning and the design of social futures* (pp. 9–37). New York: Routledge.

Nicholai, R. C. (2010). Authentic assessment for Yuuyaraq middle school students based on the Yuuyaraq curriculum. Master's thesis, University of Alaska Fairbanks. Proquest 1486006.

Norton, B. (2000). *Identity and language learning: Gender, ethnicity and educational change.* Essex, UK: Longman.

Norton, B., & Toohey, K. (Eds.) (2004). *Critical pedagogies and language learning.* Cambridge: Cambridge University Press.

Ochs, E. (1988). *Culture and language development: Language acquisition and language socialization in a Samoan village.* Cambridge: Cambridge University Press.

O'Malley, M. J., & Pierce, L. V. (1996). *Authentic assessment for English language learners: Practical approaches for teachers.* Boston: Addison-Wesley.

Orvik, J. (1975). *Four years of bilingual education: The Yup'ik language program in southwestern Alaska.* Fairbanks, AK: Center for Northern Educational Research.

Oulton, C. S. (2010). Focus on form through singing in a first grade Yugtun immersion classroom. Master's thesis, University of Alaska Fairbanks. Proquest 1486007.

Parker Webster, J., & John, T. A. (2010). Preserving a space for cross-cultural collaborations: An account of insider/outsider issues. *Ethnography and Education* 5(2), 175–91.

Parker Webster, J., Wiles, P., Civil, M., & Clark, S. (2005). Finding a good fit: Using MCC in a "third space." *Journal of American Indian Education* 44(3), 9–30.

Parker Webster, J., Yanez, E., & Andrew-Ihrke, D. (2007). *Literacy counts: A teacher's guide to developing literacies for math in a cultural context (MCC)* (pilot ed.). Fairbanks: University of Alaska.

Patrick, D. (2007). Indigenous language endangerment and the unfinished business of nation states. In A. Duchene & M. Heller (Eds.), *Discourses of endangerment: Interest and ideology in the defense of languages* (pp. 35–56). London: Continuum.

Paulston, C. B. (1994). *Linguistic minorities in multilingual settings*. Philadelphia: John Benjamins.

Pitka, M. A. (2010). Teachers guide to creating and implementing kindergarten culturally relevant learning centers. Unpublished master's project, University of Alaska Fairbanks.

Poehner, M., & Lantolf, J. (2005). Dynamic assessment in the language classroom. *Language Teaching Research* 9(3), 233–65.

Powell, M. (2002). Rhetorics of survivance: How American Indians use writing. *College Composition and Communication* 53(3), 396–434.

Pratt, M. L. (1991). Arts of the contact zone. *Profession 91*, 33–40.

Prince, T. (2010). Elder involvement through storytelling and crafts in a fourth grade Yup'ik bilingual classroom. Unpublished master's project, University of Alaska Fairbanks.

Pullar, G. (1994). The Qikertarmiut and the scientist: Fifty years of clashing world views. In T. Bray & T. Killion (Eds.), *Reckoning with the dead: The Larsen Bay repatriation and the Smithsonian Institution*. Washington, DC: Smithsonian Institution Press.

Reed, I. (1974). The Eskimo Language Workshop. In J. Orvik & R. Barnhardt (Eds.), *Cultural Influences in Alaskan Native Education*. Fairbanks, AK: Center for Northern Educational Research.

Rogoff, B. (1990). *Apprenticeship in thinking: Cognitive development in social context*. New York: Oxford University Press.

Rogoff, B. (1993). Observing sociocultural activity on three planes. In J. V. Wertsch, P. del Río, & A. Alvarez (Eds.), *Sociocultural studies of mind* (pp. 139–63). New York: Cambridge University Press.

Samson, S. P. (2010). *Yuraq*: An introduction to writing. Master's thesis, University of Alaska Fairbanks. Proquest 1486008.

Schlosser, L. Z., & Foley, P. F. (2008). Ethical issues in multicultural student-faculty mentoring relationships in higher education. *Mentoring & Tutoring: Partnership in Learning* 16(1), 63–75.

Schlosser, L. Z., & Gelso, C. J. (2001). Measuring the working alliance in advisor-advisee relationships in graduate school. *Journal of Counseling Psychology* 48, 157–67.

Seale, D., & Slapin, B. (2006). *A broken flute: The native experience in books for children*. Lanham, MD: AltaMira Press.

Siekmann, S. (2004). Mediational tool use and strategic behaviors during collaborative online reading: A microgenetic case study of beginning students of German. Doctoral dissertation, University of South Florida. *Graduate School Theses and Dissertations*, http://scholarcommons.usf.edu/etd/2959.

Siekmann, S., Marlow, P. E., & Parker Webster, J. (2008, March). Minority and heritage teacher beliefs about language education and bilingualism: Investigating a two year M.A. program for rural Alaska. Poster presented at the annual meeting of the American Association of Applied Linguistics, Washington, DC.

Siekmann, S., & Sikorski, K. (2009, March). Reinventing technology: Computers as tools for co constructing the local voice in materials development. In S. Siekmann (Chair) *(Re)claiming the Tools: Co-constructing Voice, Agency and Power.* Symposium conducted at the meeting of the American Association of Applied Linguistics, Denver, CO.

Sims, C. (2006). Language planning in contemporary American Indian pueblo communities: Contemporary challenges and issues. *Current Issues in Language Planning* 7(2–3), 251–67.

Smagorinsky, P. (1995). The social construction of data: Methodological problems of investigating learning the zone of proximal development. *Review of Educational Research* 65(3), 191–212.

Smith, L. (1999). *Decolonizing methodologies: Research and Indigenous peoples.* New York: Zed Books.

Stairs, A. (1994). The cultural negotiation of Indigenous education: Between microethnography and model-building. *Peabody Journal of Education* 69(2), 154–71.

Strauss, A., & Corbin, J. (1990). *Basics of qualitative research: Grounded theory procedures and techniques.* Newbury Park, CA: Sage.

Sundown, J. T. (2010). Using multicultural literature to promote cultural awareness and deepen understanding of your own: A Yup'ik teacher-researcher's journey. Master's thesis, University of Alaska Fairbanks. Proquest 1486009.

Swain, M. (1985) Communicative competence: Some roles of comprehensible input and comprehensible output in its development. In S. Gass & C. Madden (Eds.), *Input in second language acquisition* (pp. 235–56). New York: Newbury House.

Swain, M. (2000). The output hypothesis and beyond: Mediating acquisition through collaborative dialogue. In J. P. Lantolf (Ed.), *Sociocultural theory and second language learning* (pp. 97–114). Oxford: Oxford University Press.

Swain, M., & Johnson, R. K. (1997). Immersion education: A category within bilingual education. In R. K. Johnson & M. Swain (Eds.), *Immersion education international perspectives* (pp. 1–16). Cambridge: Cambridge University Press.

Tennant, E. A., & Bitar, J. N. (1981). *Yupik lore: Oral traditions of an Eskimo people/ Yuut qanemciit: Yupiit cayaraita qanrutkumallrit.* Bethel, AK: Lower Kuskokwim School District.

Tharp, R., & Gallimore, R. (1988). *Rousing minds to life: Teaching, learning, and schooling in social context.* Cambridge: Cambridge University Press.

Thorne, S. L. (2005). Epistemology, politics, and ethics in sociocultural theory. *Modern Language Journal* 89, 393–409.

Thorne, S. L. (2006). *New technologies and additional language learning* (CALPER Working Papers Series, No. 7). Pennsylvania State University, Center for Advanced Language Proficiency Education and Research. Available at http://calper.la.psu.edu/publication.php?page=wps7.

Tollefson, J. W. (1991). *Planning language, planning inequality: Language policy in the community.* London: Longman.

Tollefson, J. W. (2002). Introduction: Critical issues in educational language policy. In J. W. Tollefson (Ed.), *Language policies in education: Critical issues* (pp. 3–15). Mahwah, NJ: Lawrence Erlbaum.

Tripp, D. (1990). Socially critical action research. *Theory into Practice* 29(3), 158–66.

Vanderpool, E. (2010). Integrating technology and literacy to improve English reading and writing for Alaska Native students. Unpublished master's project, University of Alaska Fairbanks.

Vizenor, G. (1994a). *Manifest manners: Postindian warriors of survivance*. Hanover, NH: University Press of New England.

Vizenor, G. (1994b). *Shadow distance: A Gerald Vizenor reader*. Hanover, NH: Wesleyan University Press.

Vizenor, G. (2009). *Native liberty: Natural reason and cultural survivance*. Lincoln: University of Nebraska Press.

Vygotsky, L. S. (1962). *Thought and language*, trans. E. Hanfmann & G. Vaker. Cambridge, MA: MIT Press.

Vygotsky, L. S. (1978). *Mind in society: The development of higher psychological processes*, ed. M. Cole, V. John-Steiner, S. Scribner, & E. Souberman. Cambridge, MA: Harvard University Press.

Vygotsky, L. S. (1987). Thinking in speech. In *Collected works, 1* (pp. 39–285), ed. R. Rieber & A. Carton, trans. N. Minic. New York: Plenum (original work published 1934).

Walker, J. A. (2006). A reconceptualization of mentoring in counselor education: Using a relational model to promote mutuality and embrace differences. *Journal of Humanistic Counseling, Education, and Development*, 45, 60–69.

Wallace, S. E. (2010). Multimedia curriculum mapping: A tool for tasked based authentic second language teaching and learning through technology. Unpublished master's project, University of Alaska Fairbanks.

Wertsch, J. V. (1985). *Vygotsky and the social formation of the mind*. Cambridge, MA: Harvard University Press.

Wiget, A., (1985). *Native American literature*. Boston: Twayne.

Wilkinson, L. C., & Silliman, E. R. (2000). Classroom language and literacy learning. In M. L. Kamil, P. B. Mosenthal, P .D. Pearson, & R. Barr (Eds.), *Handbook of reading research* (vol. 3, pp. 337–60). Mahwah, NJ: Lawrence Erlbaum.

Wilson, A. C. (2004). Reclaiming our humanity: Decolonization and the recovery of Indigenous knowledge. In D. A. Mihesua & A. C. Wilson (Eds.), *Indigenizing the academy: Transforming scholarship and empowering communities*. Lincoln: University of Nebraska Press.

Wilson, S. (2008). *Research is ceremony: Indigenous research methods*. Halifax: Fernwood.

Woodbury, A. (1993). A defense of the proposition, "When a language dies, a culture dies." Proceedings of the first annual Symposium about Language and Society—Austin (SALSA). *Texas Linguistic Forum* 33, 101–29.

Woodbury, A. (1998). Documenting rhetorical, aesthetic, and expressive loss in language shift. In L. A. Grenoble & L. J. Whaley (Eds.), *Endangered languages* (pp. 234–58). Cambridge: Cambridge University Press.

Wright, S. (2004). *Language policy and language planning*. New York: Palgrave Macmillan.

Writer, J. H. (2008). Unmasking, exposing, and confronting: Critical race theory, tribal critical race theory and multicultural education. *International Journal of Multicultural Education* 10(2). Available at http://ijme-journal.org/index.php/ijme/article/view/137/226.

Wyman, L. (2012). *Youth culture and linguistic survivance*. Clevedon, UK: Multilingual Matters.

About the Editors

Patrick Marlow is Associate Professor of Linguistics at the Alaska Native Language Center and the School of Education at the University of Alaska Fairbanks. He has been a principal investigator and/or major contributor on numerous US Department of Education grants supporting Indigenous graduate and undergraduate students interested in addressing Indigenous language issues. Marlow's research and creative work seeks to understand the language planning goals of Alaska Native communities in an effort to facilitate those goals and by extension, to facilitate community ownership over language programs (both K–12 and community). His work is applied, interdisciplinary (drawing on the fields of education, linguistics, and sociology of language), and collaborative. Furthermore, his research is "critical" and seeks to empower community members to change their situation in ways that are meaningful and appropriate to them. Since 2002, Marlow has focused largely on collaborative work with Central Yup'ik communities in the Bethel area.

Sabine Siekmann is Associate Professor of Linguistics and Foreign Languages at the University of Alaska Fairbanks. She holds a PhD in second language acquisition and instructional technology and directed the Languages Resource Center at Gettysburg College. She has been a principal investigator and/or major contributor on a number of US Department of Education grants supporting Indigenous language teaching and learning through teacher professional development and materials development.

Her research focuses on applications of sociocultural theory to classroom-based language teaching and learning, including computer-assisted language learning (CALL) with an emphasis on peer mediation and activity theory. Since 2006, Siekmann has focused largely on collaborative work with Central Yup'ik communities in the Bethel area.

About the Contributors

Walkie Charles (Yup'ik) is Assistant Professor of Central Alaskan Yup'ik in the Alaska Native Language Program at the University of Alaska Fairbanks. He received his PhD in applied linguistics in 2011. His interests include dynamic assessment, sociocultural theory, and Yugtun (Yup'ik Eskimo) language teaching and learning. His dissertation was titled *Dynamic Assessment in a Yugtun L2 Intermediate Adult Classroom*.

Marilee Coles-Ritchie is Associate Professor at Westminster College, where she teaches educational foundations, qualitative research methods, and English language endorsement courses. She has experience working in the field of language acquisition and multicultural education for over twenty years. She has taught English learners in many diverse settings, including a public high school in Douglas, Arizona; a bilingual secondary school in Quito, Ecuador; and an elementary school in the Navajo Nation. She has a master's of teaching degree in TESOL (Teaching English to Speakers of Other Languages) and a PhD in cultural and social foundations of education. Her work includes collaborative action research that illustrates creative ways teachers navigate structural barriers to support students' home languages and funds of knowledge. She continues to explore how intersections of competing and conflicting discourses concerning language instruction, comprehensive teacher professional development, and measures of academic achievement impact equitable learning environments.

April G. L. Counceller (Alutiiq), also known as Isiik, is Assistant Professor of Alutiiq language and culture at Kodiak College, a campus of University of Alaska Anchorage, where she is developing an Alutiiq studies program. She serves as the language program manager for the Alutiiq Museum and Archaeological Repository, a Native-run nonprofit where she has worked since 2002. She is organizer for the Qik'rtarmiut Alutiit (Alutiiq People of the Island) Regional Language Advisory Committee and the Nuta'at Niugnelistet (New Word Makers) Alutiiq New Words Council. She sits on advisory boards for the Alaska Native Language Archive, and Cultural Survival's Native American Language program and serves on the Alaska Anthropological Association board of directors, and the Alaska Native Languages Preservation and Advisory Council. Her doctoral research centered on participant benefits of community-based language programs and refocused discourse on heritage revitalization in terms of sovereignty and self-determination.

Theresa Arevgaq John is Associate Professor in Alaska Native studies and rural development at the University of Alaska Fairbanks. John currently serves on the National Advisory Council on Indian Education and the Alaska State Council on the Arts board, and she is the former chair of the Arts Council's Traditional Native Arts Panel. She is also the recipient of the governor's Distinguished Humanities Educator Award. John is an expert on Yup'ik traditional dance, and she is herself a traditional culture bearer. Her research focuses on traditional Yup'ik song and dance and Indigenous epistemologies. It is her personal mission to collect and learn as many Yup'ik songs and dances as possible from elders before they are gone.

Joan Parker Webster is retired Associate Professor of Education at the University of Alaska Fairbanks. During her tenure, she developed the Reading Endorsement for state licensure and the master's of reading and literacy program at University of Alaska Fairbanks. Parker Webster also worked extensively with the Math in a Cultural Context project, developing literacy modules based on Alaska Native storytelling. During her last four years at University of Alaska Fairbanks, she taught in the SLATE program. She is currently an educational consultant and continues to conduct ethnographic research and write in the areas of online education, research methodologies, and multiliteracies.

Hishinlai' "Kathy R. Sikorski," received her MEd in curriculum and instruction in 2008 and is currently working on her dissertation. Her research and interests are on Indigenous language learning and teaching, second language acquisition, self-identity, sociocultural theory, and activity theory. She has worked extensively with Indigenous groups (Athabascan, Haida, Tlingit, Alutiiq, and Aleut) throughout Alaska and Canada. Hishinlai' MEd di'įį ts'à' jùk PhD geenjit ch'adantł'oo. J̀ii kwaii geenjit gineech'ahtthat—nats'àhts'à' diiginjìk geech'oorahtan, nats'àhts'à' diiginjìk gooraa'ee, ginjih ch'izhii gooraa'ee, nats'àhts'à' adagineech'arahtthat, ts'à' nats'à' diilak nąįį dèegee'yà'. Hishinlai' Dinjii Zhuh nąįį Alaska ts'à' Canada nahkat gwats'an goovaa tr'agwah'yà'.

Index